# EMAIL MASTERY!

- ✓ Get more prospects
- ✓ Convert more leads
- ✓ Orchestrate referrals

Dean Jackson

Copyright © 2013 NewInformation!, Inc

All rights reserved.

ISBN-10: 1492932809
ISBN-13: 978-1492932802

October 2013

From: Winter Haven, FL

Sunny and 82

**Welcome to Email Mastery!**

You're just minutes away from sending your very first 9-word email...and you're going to be amazed at what happens.

Here's how it works...

I developed this idea for a real estate agent client who had generated a lot of leads from their website, and got so busy they ended up neglecting a lot of the people who had responded to their ads.

They had a few hundred people who had inquired over the previous six months, and they had not been in communication with them at all.

I asked "do you know if any of them are still looking for a home?"

"I don't know" they said.

"Why don't we email them and ask?"

And that was the birth of what I call "The Amazing 9-Word Email That Revives Dead Leads"

We sent a short email to the list with only their first name in the subject line.

Subj: Jason

Are you still looking for a house in Georgetown?

That's it.

Nothing else.

Dozens of replies. Lots of engagement. Connected with a client who bought that weekend...and several others over the next couple of months.

We've sent thousands of those emails over the last few years with amazing results.

I've never seen anything like it.

This email works in all kinds of different situations.

I've seen it used in all kinds of different businesses to reconnect with anyone who inquired or downloaded a free report or information on your website.

A yacht broker sent out the message to some yacht prospects he hadn't spoken to and uncovered a buyer for a $100 Million yacht.

All the email said was "Hi Dean...Are you still looking for a yacht?"

A motorcycle jeans manufacturer in the UK sent a message that simply said "Are you still looking for stylish motorcycle jeans?" and sold over $9000 in less than a week.

There are lots and lots and lots of examples of how you can use this kind of email.

The big idea is to send an email that sounds like you just ran into them (in person) at Starbucks and you're asking them a question...expecting a response.

Short. Personal. Expecting a reply.

We want the email to seem like they are the ONLY person in the world getting this email.

It can be trickier than it sounds, because we're so used to sending out messages that sound like you're addressing a GROUP of people.

The truth is...they don't know or even care that they are part of a group. They don't know they're on your LIST. They have zero relationship with the other people on your list. They only have a relationship with YOU.

The better you get at this type of email, the more responsive and engaged your prospects and clients will be.

The temptation is to add more to it. To explain the reason you're asking.

Are you still looking for a house in Georgetown?

Because if you are...have I got a deal for you!

Don't do it. This dialogue method of email is best when you treat it exactly like a conversation. Just a really slow conversation.

You say something. They say something. You say something. Just like you are talking.

Want to try it out?

Send me an email at Dean@DeanJackson.com and show me what you come up with and lets see what happens!

I can't wait to hear about your results :)

Dean Jackson

PS - I do a free weekly podcast with Joe Polish called I Love Marketing! You can find it at ILoveMarketing.com and on iTunes. The next four chapters are full transcripts of a series of podcasts we did all about email marketing.

I've included the episode numbers if you'd rather listen to them on ILoveMarketing.com.

There are lots of advanced and ninja email strategies we use every day.

Enjoy!

# Heres's What's Inside...

Pg.

9. Episode 104
   **The One About Ninja Email Strategies**

40. Episode 105
    **The One About Even More Email Marketing**

68. Episode 106
    **The One About Ridiculously Easy Email Stratagies**

95. Episode 108
    **The One Where We Share Some Email Marketing Results**

# Episode 104
# The One About Ninja Email Strategies

Dean: Hey, everybody. It's Dean Jackson.

Joe: And Joe Polish. *The* Joe Polish.

Dean: I love that. You know what? You'd be so happy tonight, because I have, right in front of me, a bowl. And in this bowl is not chocolate-covered anything, or anything bad or liquid kind of Satan or anything. I have some fresh, delicious grapes.

Joe: Well, there are some people that will actually argue that grapes aren't all that good for you. But compared to like Cheerios or compared to something else, I guess that's pretty good. Are they organic or are they like pesticide-ridden grapes?

Dean: They are organic, green, seedless grapes. They're fantastic.

Joe: Oh, so they're those green, genetically-modified, organic grapes? I'm just messing with you.

Dean: You have to pooh-pooh everything, don't you? I was going to throwback. I was doing a throwback. You know why I said that?

Joe: Why is that?

Dean: Because I was reading, in the I Love Marketing yearbook, volume one, one of the episodes that started out with you talking about eating your organic blueberries.

Joe: Oh, okay.

Dean: So, that's a little throwback. That's a little throwback for the regular listeners. They might recognize what was happening there.

Joe: According to the latest scientific research, blueberries are probably a much better food to eat than grapes.

Dean: Okay.

Joe: But, that being said, I think this is improvement.

Dean: It's a step in the right direction. Right?

Joe: Absolutely. Absolutely. We're going to talk about glycemic index and all kinds of other things.

Dean: Welcome to the "I love my blood sugar" episode. Oh, that's so funny! Well, quit messing around, because I've got important stuff to talk about tonight. So, none of this. Quit your jibber-jabbering, and let's get right down to business.

Joe: Let's hit it. You're going to talk about crazy results that people have been getting using the magic 9-word email.

Dean: Well, that's part of it. We haven't done an episode about email marketing in a long time – if ever – exclusively about email. So, I was thinking this would probably be a good time for us to do that, especially on the heels of seeing all of these results that have been coming back here.

Joe: You know, it's so funny how people have discussions like, "Does anyone use direct mail anymore?" Does anyone still use email? There are new things like Facebook and Twitter.

Dean: That's old-school. Nobody uses those anymore. It's all texting, Joe. It's all texting. It's all about the texting.

Joe: Oh, my god. Oh, wait! I've got to tell you something. I literally went and saw Jay Leno do a live event last night, and I got backstage passes because a friend introduced me to Bernard, took me down to Jay Leno's garage a few months ago, so I had a meeting with Jay backstage, beforehand, to see if I could get him to speak at the 25K annual meeting that we're doing this year. But he's filming during that time, so he can't actually speak at it during those dates, which is a drag.

But, part of his skit, he was talking about the Steve Jobs biography, the book, and basically one of the last things that Steve was working on was an iPad where you actually move your hands. You don't have to touch it, and it would actually do what you needed to do.

So, he did this really funny skit where he said, "You know, could you imagine? Before technology, you knew who the crazy people were. They were the ones that were just kind of like walking, and they would be moving their hands and making gestures, and doing crazy shit." He's like, "Now, you just never even know, because before, when you'd see someone with a Bluetooth, they would be talking to themselves. When Bluetooth first came out, you thought they had Tourette's, because they're like yelling and screaming." But he goes, "Now, you have all these people waving their arms back and forth, and in circles and everything, and you just never know what the hell's going on anymore, with technology."

I thought that was kind of amusing.

My whole point behind all of that was that I think direct mail is the new thing. I think we've talked about this on a past episode.

But that being said, we have not done a whole episode just about this. So, I'm just going to sit back and listen to you talk the whole time. The last episode, I think I pretty much talked most of the time.

Dean: I think it set some kind of new record for the ratio. It's perfect. It was a pretty easy episode for me.

Joe: It was. You were probably drinking and smoking and eating grapes.

Dean: Drinking, smoking, and eating grapes. I like it. That's funny.

Do you ever get any email?

Joe: Of course. I get way too much. I think email is like one of the biggest annoyances on the planet. Which, of course, the point behind saying that is for the best uses of email, you can use it, just don't be used by it, although I think most everyone is used by it, if you even have it.

Dean: Do you know what I heard the other day?

Joe: What's that?

Dean: I think it was Brendon who said that your email in-box is a fantastic tool for other people to prioritize your time.

Joe: Yeah. Yeah.

Dean: Was that Brendon that said that?

Joe: I've heard him say stuff similar to that, so I would very much say that was something he would say.

Dean: It's a perfect tool for other people to organize and prioritize your time.

Joe: Right. Well, part of it is do you use it or do you get used by it? If you're going to have it, you're better off using it for your own benefit, than being used by it. And, certainly, it's an awesome tool.

See, every form of communication is awesome. Reading a book was awesome, when books first came out. And part of it is what side are you on? Are you the one who's profiting from the use of it, or are you just the one that's consuming it? Are you the one that's being bombarded by it?

I can't remember who said it, but I heard Denny Hatch talk about this quote. I don't think it was Denny Hatch's quote. But it was basically, "Direct marketing, you have to get through with the clutter with an offer that is so interruptive, that it keeps on interrupting until action is taken."

I heard him say that before email even existed, to most human beings. Today, that same saying applies. You have to get through the clutter with an offer that just makes sense, that's simple, that speaks to the person, and that sort of stuff.

Dean: Right. Part of the thing, and let's kind of begin right at the beginning here, with our discussion about email marketing, because I really do believe that it is the power tool, it is the tool for marketers, if you use it properly.

If you use it in the right way, if you use it like you can, so often what I find is that people come into it with the wrong idea. They either try and get it to do too much, or they're trying to do too much at once, and they're not really using it in a way that capitalizes on the ability for email to be a tool for dialogue, a conversation.

You really want to know that what you've got is the ability to have an interactive dialogue where different things happen, depending on how the response goes.

Now, we've talked before about some of the email things that we do. We've talked about the amazing 9-word email that revives dead leads, and I'll talk about that in a second. But what I want to do is talk about the psychology that is in play before you even push the send button, and to really get that right, to understand what it is.

I often say to people they don't know what they want it to do. They don't know what their objective is. So, the most important thing is to really begin with the end in mind. And beginning with the end in mind means knowing who is it that we're speaking to, and what is it, what's the verb, what's the action, the outcome that we want to have happen as a result of sending this email, and realizing what the opportunities are and what the limitations are of email marketing, of sending email in the first place.

So, I always really like to think about the environment that's surrounding somebody checking their email. If you really think about it, if we begin with the end in mind, we begin with how it's going to actually be received, most people now tend to check their email on their iPhone, they're checking it all the time, they're checking it on their iPad. It's not very often that you can't reach somebody by email pretty quickly, if you wanted to.

I think even though people have aspirations of checking their email once a day or twice a day, or 3 times a day, I don't think that's the reality for most people. Do you think so? What do you do with your email?

Joe: Where I am currently in my life, and this is always an aspiration, in an ideal world, I would have chunks of time where I would check email. I would have days that would go by that I didn't check it at all. I'd be lying if I said I've been able to do any of those things really well. Maybe for small periods of time.

There was a period of time, a couple of years ago, where I literally did not check email for like a month, and it was one of the hardest damn things I've ever had to do. On one hand, it was extremely relieving. But on the other, the emails were going to an assistant, and they'd still get brought up to me, printed out and stuff like that. So, I'm really not checking it.

So, to answer your question, I check it throughout the day. With an iPhone, which I carry, there's that magnetic, addictive force. And since I already have that sort of addict brain anyway, it's really hard for me to restrain. If I go somewhere and don't want to check email, I just literally have to turn the phone off, so I'm not even drawn.

But, there is a compulsive poltergeist that's built into electronic devices, that just hijacks your brain and makes you want to look at these things.

Now, to give you another example of this, though, I wanted to do a test. I shouldn't even mention it, but I will because I think it's funny.

I thought of the power of an irresistible offer. Before I went and saw Jay Leno, yesterday, I sent an email to Richard Branson and also to Peter Diamandis. I said, "I'm going to go meet with Jay Leno tonight. Do you want to be on the show? Do you have any interest in being on the show?"

Now, Richard, sometimes I'll send Richard an email and I won't hear back from him. Sometimes it's the same day, other times it can be days. And there will be a couple of times, depending on how busy he is, he won't respond at all because he misses it or whatever.

But I'll tell you, both of them responded back immediately, "Yes, I'd like to be on Jay Leno's show."

So, what's funny is that with the right offer, no matter who they are, including billionaires, they will respond, quickly, if they're looking at it.

I said to Eunice, "You know what? Us marketers are so right about an irresistible offer. It doesn't matter who the person is." And it was a simple, short email. "Would you like to be on Jay Leno?"

When I talked to Jay, he's like, "Yeah, have him contact our people," that sort of stuff. But the thing is I think most people are constantly looking at their emails. And we have a few friends, like you have Dan Kennedy, who doesn't use email at all.

Dean: I know. Never, at all. Do you want to know something spooky?

Joe: What's that?

Dean: "Richard, would you like to be on Jay Leno" is a 9-word email. Maybe there is something magic to 9 words.

Joe: That's funny. I'm sitting here counting with my fingers. This is how stupid I am. We're sitting here doing a broadcast.

Dean: But, it is. It's 9 words. I counted it on my fingers, too.

Joe: That is funny.

Dean: It is pretty funny, but you are absolutely right. So, let me ask you this. How long was it between when you sent that message to Richard and he responded?

Joe: Do you want me to actually get the actual time? Hold on.

Dean: Just ballpark. Was it the same day? Was it within an hour?

Joe: No, I think it was easily within an hour.

Dean: Yeah, within an hour. So, there's the thing.

Joe: I'm going to try to go through it. I don't want to do it on my computer, because it interrupts the recording while we're doing it.

Dean: No, no. Don't do that. That's all I wanted to know.

Joe: I might be able to do it from my iPhone. I can check my email while we're talking about email.

Dean: There we go. But listen, the point is that it wasn't 3 days. It was literally almost instantaneously. Right?

Joe: Right.

Dean: Okay, so you've stumbled on something – that this is part of the thing. So, there's one thing. Now, this is part of the really deep psychology of what's going on here. So, the elements that make that work is he knows who you are, first off.

Joe: Yeah. Most people can't email Richard Branson because they don't have his email. And secondly, if he doesn't know

|  |  |
|---|---|
|  | Even the magic 9-word email would work for online dating, if someone wanted to get dates. |
| Dean: | It works for anything. I've got so much more stuff. So, next time, we'll share more about it. But I think this is a good start. |
| Joe: | Yeah, that's it. So, I'm going to go to dinner. We've now gone over time, so we've not been respectful of anyone's time. Can't ask for a refund, because it's a free podcast. But what do you do, right? |
| Dean: | You know, we went short a little last week, so this will make up for it. |
| Joe: | If you're brand new to our podcast, welcome to the club, ILoveMarketing.com. If you're listening on iTunes, go to the website. You can download your free report, Breakthrough DNA. And if you've already read our report, Breakthrough DNA, 42 times, it isn't going to hurt you to read it another 43 times. |
| Dean: | Amen. |
| Joe: | I don't know if that made sense, but that's it. |
| Dean: | It does. Perfect. |
| Joe: | Okay, bye. |
| Dean: | Yes. Bye. |

them, yeah. You've got to have rapport with him.

Dean: Somehow, you got the email that he checks. That's all I'm saying. It doesn't even matter whether you know him or not. I'm sure the email that you have isn't the email that everybody in the world gets for Richard Branson.

Joe: No, no. It's his personal email.

Dean: It's his personal email, and that's the thing. If you've got somebody's personal email, you have a very intimate connection to that person. And I say intimate meaning that you sort of have inside access, no matter what else is going on, no matter where he is.

You're saying this magnetic draw of checking your email, of always seeing what's going on. He could be with the queen, and when he slips into the bathroom or something, he's got his phone with him and is checking it while he's out of their sight.

Everybody's like that. That's what happens. So, you have kind of intimate access to somebody.

When you look at your email, do you think, at the time that he looked at that email, it was the only email in his in-box?

Joe: No. There were probably tons.

Dean: No. So, what happens when you scan through this? It's even more relevant that the email in-box is equally treated the same way, as Gary Halbert talked about, with people sorting their mail over the garbage. The A-pile and the B-pile. Right?

Joe: Uh-huh.

Dean: I think what happens there is I think that there's kind of like 3 levels of it that are going on. People skim their email, because they come in bulk and you can't stop them. They come so fast. You maybe check your email, and there are

20 new ones since the last time you checked, even if you're checking pretty often.

So, most people now are using gmail and probably don't delete emails. I don't really delete anything. Do you?

Joe: Yeah, I do. I actually switched back to Outlook, believe it or not, on a Mac. We still have gmail, and I don't delete them. I started deleting them. That's one thing I couldn't stand about gmail, is I just kept them all, like 60,000 freaking emails.

Dean: I love it, because as long as you know it's in there, you can find it, search it. I like that a lot.

Most people, it's not really about deleting. It's not like you've got this backlog of emails all piling up on your computer, on your hard drive, when it was like limited space and you had to delete your email so you could run one of your programs or something. It's not like that anymore.

Joe: Speak for yourself. Even my gmail account is like at the limit. I would always have to go and delete it, because it would get so big.

Dean: I bought some more storage, so, yeah.

Joe: I bought the maximum storage that they will even allow.

Dean: Oh, I see what you're saying.

Joe: Currently.

Dean: It's not so much about the email being deleted. People are skimming the emails. The big decision is, really, one of 3 things: "Am I going to open this? Am I going to read this? Or am I going to respond to this?" I think those are really the 3 things that you really want.

The only thing that's going on in the subject line and the from line is people making the decision of whether they're going to open it or not. That's the only thing.

I don't know whether I read the subject line first or whether I read whom it's from. I think I read the subject line first, and then I look over and see whom it's from.

So, if it's a subject line that looks like a personal email, like the equivalent of Gary Halbert's idea of a personal letter, that's going to get some great attention. Right?

If it's clearly a tagline or teaser copy in the subject line, it tips me off that I know it's not like somebody just sending it to me. And if it comes from a company or comes from a website as the from line, I know that it's not a personal thing.

So, you know, going into it, which ones you're going to scan. You have kind of your A-list, you've got your personal emails, your friends and associates and people that you want to hear from or frequently hear from. When you decide to open it, then the thing is what am I going to do with this? Am I going to read it?

When you look at like the first thing that you have to do is turn images on or you click here if this email's not displaying properly, all those things tip you off that this is not an email from a person to one person.

That's why when I look at these, I never am sending graphic emails. And I say, "Graphic," because sometimes I'll say, "I never send html emails," but you can send html-coded emails but not graphic emails that have pictures and logos and all that kind of stuff on them, to get the most response.

When you preview the beginning of it, you can see that the first words are "turn images on," or whatever, as the first words in the email, when you look at it in that preview window, that kind of lets people know that this is not a personal communication.

So, if you just look at those first 2 things, if you look at the emails that you actually respond to, they're going to be emails that are from somebody that you know, from somebody that you wouldn't be surprised to have a dialogue from. Even if it is somebody that's asking you a question, a question is really one of those magnetic things that sort of demands some attention. You have to willfully decide to ignore somebody, if you're not going to answer a question, if all of those other things fall into place.

Think about the emails that you send to people that you know. Emails that we send back and forth are very rarely more than 2 or 3 lines, because they're a utility. They're sending something; you're expecting a reply.

So, when I look at these, the elements that I have discovered that are the winning formula for email are to send emails that are short, personal, and expecting a reply. And if you can get those 3 elements in the email, you have something that almost has the potential to be magical.

It's really interesting. You know, Joe, our friend Kim White, from Austria. When we were doing our email for the I Love Marketing conference, I sent out an email to subscribers that had just their first name in the subject line.

Now, if you see an email like that, that's going to get your attention. That's an email that is going to kind of draw your eyes. It's proven, when they do all kinds of studies, that your name, when you see it in print or when you see it in an email, your eyes dilate and you're gravitated towards it. It's kind of like when you hear your name. But when you see it, they've done all kinds of eye-tracking surveys that show that your eyes are actually attracted to it and your eyes dilate. It's almost like getting those little squirts of dopamine. There's something that, "That's me!" You have that identity to it.

It doesn't have to just be their name, but something that is going to get their attention in a personal way.

But when I sent out that email, I sent it out, and the subject line was just, "Kim." And then, the email itself was just a simple email. "Hi, Kim! Are you planning on coming to the I Love Marketing conference next month? Dean."

You remember when we sent out those emails? That was all it was. That was the end of the email. And Kim responded and said that he wasn't going to be able to because he was in Austria and whatever else.

But when I saw him, I saw him a few weeks later, when we were in Toronto. I think you were there, too. He said to me, "That email that you sent," he said, "I thought that was like a personal email to me." But he had to come up and confirm with me that it was a broadcast email, because he looked back at it and saw, piecing it together, that this was an autoresponder.

But the immediate thing, his immediate thought and the words that he said to me was that, "The energy of that email was very different than other emails that you get."

Kim, we should probably describe what Kim does. But Kim is an energy worker. Is that what you would call him? How would you describe what he does?

Joe: Well, Dan Sullivan refers to him as a spiritual plumber.

Dean: Spiritual plumber. That's right.

Joe: But, what does that mean? I have no idea.

Dean: Dan talks about Kim. You know how when you have some relationship with people or something or somebody just kind of like irks you or there's some negative energy around it where you're in some kind of argument or you've got some kind of negative energy around that relationship?

Joe: Animosity. Sort of like what we share with each other outside of doing this I Love Marketing podcast?

Dean: Yeah. Often. Often, I've thought about calling Kim a couple of times.

So, what Kim will do is he can work with you and he can sort of remove that energy. Dan is, incredibly, a fan of him. He talks about him all the time.

So, for him, as an energy worker, to say there's something about – because we had a whole discussion then – the energy of the email, and I think that part of it is that the energy of an email like that is that my intention, my pure intention from that email is that I wanted it to feel like an email from one person to one person. And I truly did want it to be an email from me to them, a personal email.

I say that because even though you're sending out an email to thousands or tens of thousands, or hundreds of thousands of people, they're only being read one person at a time.

So, often, people – in the language that they use – the way that they word the email, the tone of the email is speaking to a group. It's kind of broadcasting or announcing. It's the difference between getting up onstage and presenting your email to the entire room, versus taking somebody aside in the hall and having the communication with them one person at a time.

That is a very big distinction, and you don't have to use email as a broadcast tool.

Now, sometimes it makes sense because, often, we send out broadcasts where we just want to get a message out to everybody. Not every email needs to be short, personal, and expecting a reply. Sometimes, sending out emails for the purpose of communicating information to a group is great. And that's what really makes the short, personal, and expecting a reply emails so powerful, is that you sparingly use them when it's your intention, when you really want that to happen, when you want somebody to respond to something. When you want them to take an individual action at the highest rates possible, you have to communicate with them one person at a time.

So, when I asked you, sharing these behind-the-scenes things of how your email works, of what you do when you're checking your email, and really kind of painting the picture, getting the environment of how people engage with their email, we're doing it alone. Nobody is like, "Hey, everybody, let's gather around and check my email." That's not the way people do email. They don't check it in a group. And nobody prints them off and reads them aloud to the group. "Hey, everybody, I got another one! Listen to this one!" That's not the way that we interact with email. And it sounds funny when I say it like that, but you've got to imagine that that's often the way people are writing their email. They're writing it as if people are going to be gathering around and having it read to them. Does that make sense?

Joe: Yeah, it makes total sense. Let me ask you a question. We'll probably talk to this, but I want to make sure we bring it up.

When you're sending out emails, I'm sure it changes and I don't even know, the unsubscribe, do you know the legalities on that, like when you're sending out emails?

Dean: Well, you always have the unsubscribe. You have to. But what you don't have to do is make it the prominent thing. It's always there. It's always there. And you're not trying to hide it, or you're not trying to mask it or not include it. It doesn't matter.

But when you're looking at the email, there's nothing wrong with having a little separation between your message and the unsubscribe portion of the email. You can do that. There are lots of different things that you can do where you are making your message the prominent thing.

So, I'm saying this because I want to be really careful with the way that I say it.

The only person that you should be sending email to, in the first place, is somebody who has invited you to send it, by sending it to an opt-in list, somebody who has asked for something or somebody who has voluntarily given you permission to email them.

We're not talking about scraping emails or doing things like compiled lists, and all that kind of stuff, all the other kind of spammy kind of things, things that are where you have a context for communicating with them.

And that's why a smaller list of people who actually want to hear from you is far more powerful than a giant list of people whose emails you've captured or scraped somehow.

Joe: Say someone is brand new in business. They have 10 clients. You're going to send a personal email, versus you put it into a database and start sending it that way, via Infusion or Aweber, Constant Contact, Sales Force, or whatever....

Dean: Top Clients, all of those. Right.

Joe: Do you have a rule of thumb? Because certainly, sending something to someone that knows you, that's a personal, individual email, onesie-twosie, versus even doing a group, you're increasing your chances of a higher response.

Dean: Oh, absolutely, you are.

Now, here's the thing. I would always recommend using an autoresponder or an email broadcaster. But the way I think about it is that I use the tool to do what I would do if I could count on me to do it. I think about it that I'm sending one email to 25,000 people, instead of sending... No, it's the other way around. I'm thinking that I'm sending one email to 25,000 individuals, rather than sending one email to a group of 25,000 people.

Joe: When's the last time you sent 25,000 emails to a single person?

Dean: Hey, Joe! Hey, Joe! Hey, Joe! Hey, Joe!

Joe: Can you imagine?

Dean: Maybe for your birthday next year.

Joe: Right.

Dean: Perfect.

Joe: That is comedy.

Dean: That's very funny. I'm thinking that I'm sending one email, and I'm writing the email as if it's only one person who's going to be reading it.

And that's why when I go through all of this stuff, it sounds like we haven't even really gotten to the content of the emails, of what's the best language and what's the best thing to say, because so much of it, if you can get these things right, if you can get the psychology of why those emails work so well and why you should send short, personal, expecting-a-reply emails, it's going to make the emails that you write so much more powerful.

Joe: Yeah. I totally know.

Dean: I just think it's perfect, that you sent a 9-word email to Richard Branson and Peter Diamandis and got responses in less than an hour. But that's exactly how it works. And that's why a guy whose business is energy is saying how that email had the energy and intention of it being a personal email.

This is not easy. I'm not saying that it's easy your first time. Even though those emails are very short, I'll often spend a lot of time wordsmithing those emails. It takes time to make an email seem like you just sat down and fired it off.

Joe: By the way, one of the things I want to be careful is making the assumption that someone that's listening to this right now has already heard our past episodes, including where we talked about everything. We had one episode where you first introduced the 9-word email, the magic 9-word email, and they can find that.

Dean: Let me tell that story, real quick, because I want people to understand what the context of email is, too. When I'm talking about email marketing things, I'm talking about a before unit email. Typically, those emails are sent to people who are sitting in profit activator #3, educate and motivate. You've gone through the work and you've identified your target market, your single target market in profit activator #1. You've done whatever it is that you're going to do to compel them to identify themselves. This is where you're going to compel them to come to a landing page and leave their name and their email for whatever it is that you're offering. You're going to then have this pool of people who are now sitting in profit activator #3, which is where all the gold is in your before unit. This is where it all happens, because once you gather those people there, now you can patiently and systematically educate and motivate them to do something when they're ready, at their own pace, at their time.

You can do so much. You can communicate with people, you can educate them, you can send, every week, some kind of valuable updates to them, you can invite them to come and listen to your podcast every week. Those are all part of the education process, where you're kind of giving them valuable content. You're adding value to them.

And then, when it comes time for you to make an offer, for you to take the lead and to initiate something where you are going to lead somebody to a better outcome that's good for them and that you know where it is that you want them to go, you know what your offer is.

I'll give you some examples of it. For real estate buyers, here are a couple examples. We'll do things like we'll run AdWord ads on Google. Every time somebody searches for real estate in Winter Haven or homes for sale in Winter Haven, or any of those things that somebody who would be looking for a home would do, we compel them to come to the website. And when they get there, they see all of these things that they can get free, inside, more inside, and they choose to leave their name and their email address.

Now, that's profit activator #2 at work. We've compelled them to identify themselves. We've taken an invisible prospect and we've made them visible. And now, all of those email addresses that we have, everybody who has come to the site and left their name and their email address is sitting there, waiting for us to start that education and motivation process in profit activator #3.

So, the way that we use email to do that is that every single week, we send them a market watch newsletter, an email, with all of the new listings that have come on the market in the last week, with links where they can see all of those properties, with little dialogue where Julie Matthews is talking about the types of homes that she's showing, the people that she's working with right now, maybe highlighting a property that she has seen, and then making an offer on that email.

We talk about how we know that what we know what buyers are going to want to do is they're either going to be driven by they want to go look at homes and we've got an offer for them, or they're going to want to get their financing all straightened out and know what that's all about. Some people are motivated by that before they want to go look at homes. And some people may just want to know what the prices are and what's going on, what they can get for their money.

So, we know, every single week, in those emails, we're including our super-signature, which is in the PS or below the PS of the email, the offers that you have for people to take advantage of.

So, if we know that they want to look at homes, we don't want them to have to take the initiative and say, "Hey, would you show me some homes?" Nobody likes to take initiative. So, we make an offer. We say, "Join us for a daily tour of homes. We do tours of homes every day, at 10:00 and 1:00." If you'd like to join us, just click here." It's a great way to homes in any area in Winter Haven. And people click on that, and they pick the tour time, and they join right in, because we're crystal clear on what we want them to do. And the reason that we're able to make that offer is because we know what they want. We've thought through what their next step is. They want to look at homes, but they don't want you to go out of your way. So, we make it seem like they can just jump on this tour.

Some people may want to know how much they can afford, but they're afraid to get a pre-approval. Pre-approval sounds scary. It sounds like your approval is going to be put into question.

So, we position that, and we talk about a free home loan report, which sounds like it's already done, or it sounds like there's a voyeuristic element to it, where I'm going to get to see all of this information. It's not that I'm being examined, it's that I'm now getting access to examine all of these loans.

So, we talk about the home loan report, and we monitor hundreds of loan programs all across the country, to find the lowest interest rate loans, the lowest total cost loans, the lowest payment loans, and we put all that together and put our findings together in our free home loan report.

People click, and they can read about that and sign up for the home loan report, because it sounds like it's already going on.

Some people may be just getting started, and they don't know, yet, what they can get for their money. So, we offer the free guide to Winter Haven real estate prices, with pictures and profiles and maps and community information – all the stuff that somebody would want to know about Winter Haven – and they're happy that somebody has taken the time to do this.

So, we make all these offers in that super-signature, but each week, when we send out the market watch email, we're highlighting one of them. So, after we say, "It's been a busy week in Winter Haven. Here are some of the new homes that I got a chance to look at. Here's the links for all the new homes that have come on the market in the last week. And if you're going to be in town this week, and you'd like to look at some homes, we do daily tours of homes at 10:00 and 1:00. It's easy to join us. Just click here, pick the tour time that you want, and we'll do all the rest."

And that's really a very simple type of email formula for sending an educational email every week.

Now, it's clear, because we use language at the top that kind of shows that this is the market watch report and it's got all of the date and from Winter Haven, and the weather, and all that kind of lead-in stuff, so people are clear that it has a newsletter feel to it. It doesn't feel like I'm the only one getting this email.

But, if we send that out to you today, and then tomorrow we send you an email that is an "re:" of that email that I sent you and includes that email that I sent you yesterday, but at the very top of it, it asks you a simple question and says, "Hi, Joe, are you an investor or are you looking for a house to live in? Julie," that is a very simple email that gets incredible response.

Now, the reason is because it seems like this email is only intended for me, and it absolutely is. It absolutely is only intended for you, even though 2,500 people are getting that email. It doesn't matter how many people get it; it's how many people are reading it at once. Right? So, people respond to that email.

Now, it's short, it's personal, it's expecting a reply.

And if you send emails like that, you are going to get more response than you've ever gotten to any emails that you've ever sent.

But that's not the end of it. It's not just about sending out an email that gets people to respond. Now, you have to skillfully, like a chess master, know where this is headed. You have to know what the end game is. You have to know what's going to happen when somebody replies to that email. And the reason that it's so responsive is that it's not immediately clear where that's going. We're not solving the mystery for them. I'm not saying, "Hey, Joe, are you an investor or are you looking for a house to live in? Because if you're an investor, I would recommend that you blah, blah, blah, blah, blah." I've solved the mystery for you.

So, part of getting people to respond is knowing that you're not going to solve the mystery yet, and know that you're going to engineer the situation so that you know what to reply, no matter what they reply.

So, when you send out an email like that, and people say, "Yes, I am an investor," we know that 95% of the people that get that email are not investors. They're looking for a house. But, of all the questions that you could ask somebody, and I spent a lot of time and still do spend a lot of time thinking and crafting emails that are really engineered to get the most response but to get a purposeful response, to get a response that I know is going to lead somewhere.

There's an element to maybe what attorneys would do in questioning witnesses. There's different kinds of questions that are in examination and cross-examination, that they ask a line of questioning, knowing that it's not just the one question that they're going to ask, but they're asking a question that the answer to it is going to determine what the next question is.

If you can patiently engineer something that will get to where you want to go in 3 moves, then you're really onto something. That's what we're really looking at. And the value of being able to sort these types of things, I look at it that one of the types of questions that we ask is a sorting question, this or that. "Are you an investor, or are you looking for a house to live in?" That kind of question is going to get one or the other type of response.

We did this with Vince DelMonte, asking people, "Are you looking to lose fat or gain muscle?" Sorting. We're sorting people into that, because if people come to a fitness site, you don't know what their intention is.

But, you can find out. What would be valuable for you to know? How do you want to steer that question?

Joe: I want to do a test to his list that says, "Are you looking to lose muscle and gain fat?" and just see what happens.

Dean: I'll text Vince. I'll get him to test that, put that in the queue.

Joe: I'm just curious.

Dean: Are you looking to lose muscle or gain fat? That's perfect.

Joe: Exactly. That one's even better than mine. See, the subtle difference is what makes all the difference. Little hinges swing big doors.

Dean: It's my 10,000 hours.

Joe: Alright, continue on. You know what I've always noticed? I'm always the timekeeper of these damned podcasts. You never like say, "Oh, being respectful of all of our listeners..." You don't go there. You spout out all these brilliant marketing ideas, but you don't care about anyone's time on this free podcast that no one's paying us for.

Dean: I know that we've been talking for 53:20, right now.

Joe: 33 seconds.

Dean: I'm fully aware of the time. I just don't feel the need to take

| | |
|---|---|
| | their time to tell them what the time is. I'd rather add value. |
| Joe: | I gotcha. Well, you've got a little less than 7 minutes to add some serious value here. |
| Dean: | And I might go long. What do you think of that? |
| Joe: | That won't work for me. |
| Dean: | It won't work for you. Oh, okay. Then, we'll try and do it in 7 minutes, for you. |
| Joe: | Go for it. |
| Dean: | And then, everyone will know that it was you that caused them to not get the full answer here. |
| Joe: | No, no. |
| Dean: | If you can think that through, knowing that that dialogue method of email is going to get the most response that you're really going to get, I want to know, from each individual person. Like I almost get to the point where it's not uncommon to send emails that get 60+% response, because you've sent it to one very specific person from one person. |

There's something powerful about that. But knowing where that's going to go.

So, if you take that example from the Ritzers, if they respond that they're an investor, now you can go down that whole investor line of questioning where you can say, "Perfect! Are you looking to buy and hold or something to fix and flip?"

So now, you're asking another sorting question, something that's going to kind of get them down that path, where you're getting into a dialogue with them. Part of the reason, I think, that people respond to those emails so much is, often, even just morbid curiosity to see is this really a personal email. Even if they think, in the back of their mind, "This might be an autoresponder, or is this person really sending it to me?" that when you send the second reply that was an intelligent response based on what they responded to the first question, now you've got their attention because now they feel like, "Oh, this really is live. This is really somebody."

What you'll find is that after about 3 or 4 of those emails, where you're kind of going back and forth like this, you'll get what I call the "love letter." The love letter is the email where they just tell you everything that you need to know or everything that they want you to know, because they now feel like they have the ear of somebody who cares and somebody who is in a position to really help them.

So, if somebody's going down that path as an investor, "Perfect! Are you looking to buy and hold or fix and flip?" And they'll say, "Well, we're looking for deals to fix and flip," "Perfect! Have you seen this one and this one?"

We now are suggesting things to them. You're demonstrating your expertise in that, and it just so happens that Julie is an investor herself and buys and flips a lot of homes, so she knows the homes that are best suited for that. She can point them out, point them in the right direction like that, and now people will give you their feedback on that and start to say, "Well, yeah, that one right there might be something. Here's what we're really looking for."

And now, you're completely engaged in a dialogue with somebody who, just a couple of hours ago, was just a number, an email on a list of people getting all of these weekly updates, where they're going to everybody. They're just sitting in the crowd.

Joe: Yeah. Totally.

Dean: I already know we're going to have to do another episode on this. I can already tell.

Joe: Is there any other choice?

Dean: I can't wrap it up in 2 minutes. We've got a cliffhanger episode, Joe.

Let's tie this one together, though. Here's what I want people to take away from this episode: to realize and, when they're approaching email marketing, to understand and really strive to use it as a tool that it's absolutely best-suited for, which is dialogue communication.

I painted that picture of where are you when you get your email and how we go through and sort our emails, and everybody can relate to that, about how people actually interact with their email and what they're going to do with it, knowing that the first thing they have to do is get it opened. They have to click on it to actually see the email, and then you want them to take that next step.

When you understand what that next step is, you can be completely focused on just that result. What's the one thing?

This is so ridiculous, but this is actually how I explain it and think to people. I say to people, "Imagine if you were a powerful wizard, and you had the power to just get anybody to do anything you suggested, and you could just type it in invisible ink? And whatever they saw, they would just do what you say."

You could literally, in the subject line, say, "Open this email," and people would open it. And when they get to the next thing, say, "Click on this link," and they would click on that link. Or, "Answer this question," or whatever it is that you want them to do.

And, really, there's only 2 things that you can get

them to do in an email, that is perfectly suited for you. You can get them to click on a link or hit reply. Those are the 2 actions that you want with an email.

Most people, if you were to look at their email, you would, crystal clearly, see that they don't have any idea what the purpose is of that email, why they're sending it, what it is that they want them to do.

When they realize that you're not going to convince somebody, they say, "Well, I want people to buy," but are they going to buy right from that email? You want them to go somewhere, and they're going to buy from that page. That's where your buy button is. That's where your shopping cart is. Right?

So, it's not about sending your web page to them through email. It's about getting them and compelling them to come to your web page.

We're at one minute over. Can I tell one more story?

Joe: Yeah. Go for it.

Dean: So, here's an example of that – a perfect example.

We do the postcard guys in Sarasota that do all of my postcard mailings, and we have a program together called "Getting Listings Sold." And we send out emails, we get all of the data of all of the new listings that come on the market, and they were sending emails to these people that were HTML, beautiful, graphic emails, sending and explaining to people who they were and all the experience that they had in postcards, and presenting the whole case for people to buy postcards right from the email.

They track and test everything beautifully. So, they're testing and tracking. They had 3 emails that they were split-testing, and one of them they were happy because they had gone from 3% click-through to 5% click-through with this new email.

So, I came in and we crafted an email that gets over 30% click-through.

And then, if they don't click, we send it again, and it gets another 30%. So, we get over 50% of the people who we send these emails to, to click on the email. And all we did, Joe, was imagine that we're sending one email to one person.

If you're a real estate agent and you get a new listing, let's say you listed 22 Graystone, and you go to bed and wake up in the morning, and you're checking your email, and in the subject line of one of those emails are just the words "22 Graystone," that's going to jump to your attention. Right? Because it could be somebody inquiring about your new listing. That's what it could be. It's certainly about 22 Graystone. And you're all excited about it, because you just got that new listing.

Now, instead of – when you click on that email – having this beautiful HTML graphic-loaded email and presenting a whole case for sending Just Listed postcards, all we did, I wrote just a very short email and said, "Hi, Joe. I put together some marketing ideas for 22 Graystone. Take a look and let me know what you think." And then, we put a link that said, "22 Graystone," and signed it Ramona, which is who was sending and who would be responding to those emails.

That email immediately went from 5% click-through to over 30% click-through because it had all of those elements and used the dynamics that are going on when people are reading their email.

Joe: What more could you ask for?

Dean: I've got so much more to say.

Joe: No, no. I mean seriously. What more could someone

even...? This is as good as it gets.

Dean: But when you think about it, if you know what it is, like I know, when I say to you, "If you were a powerful wizard, what would you put in the subject line?" the only thing that matters in the subject line is "Open this email." That's really the essence of what it is.

That's the naked truth of what you want that subject line to say. And you probably get more people to open an email that said, "Open this email," than some of the subject lines that we see. Right? You just overtly said it.

Joe: Yeah. "Open this email, real quickly."

Dean: The trick is not to just use those words, "Open this email." What you want to do is what are the most compelling words that are going to get that result? That's the only purpose of the subject line, "Open this email."

And then, when they get it, you want to know what is the outcome. Do you want somebody to respond? And if you want them to respond, then you ask them a question. Do you want them to go to another website? Do you want them to click on a link? Then you just say whatever you need to say, whatever they would find compelling, all cheese, to click on that link.

Joe: Totally. Awesome. One thing, too, you need to be congruent on what it is you're saying. For instance, we used the Jay Leno example to Branson. I've seen some people that will send out emails with a subject line like, "Want to be on Oprah?" from people that have never been on Oprah and that have no possibility of getting somebody on Oprah.

So, part of it is you want to be congruent with what it is that you're doing, because there are ways that you can say things that will get people to, obviously, respond.

Dean: You're absolutely right. You're absolutely right. Let's start the next episode with that.

Joe: Want to be on Oprah? Okay, cool. What I will also say, since I talked about Leno, the show is awesome. It was way better than what I even expected it to be. He's a really hardworking dude. And the big takeaway that I got as a business lesson is here's a guy that, according to Wikipedia, he makes like $25-million a year on The Tonight Show, and he makes another $20-million doing standup.

From seeing him, I think he's missed like 2 shows in 17 or 20 years, or whatever, since he's been on, because he was sick. The guy is so consistent. He's such a professional. It's interesting to read his Wikipedia page.

But, basically, the big takeaway is that he's always performing to keep himself sharp, even when he doesn't need to. And he's figured out how to make his performances be almost equal to the money he makes from his real job on The Tonight Show.

It really made me think about you're talking about learning this and being a wizard. The fact is what we're delivering to people, if we charged $1,000 per episode, it would be worth it, because what we're sharing has made millions and millions of dollars for people through our contests.

So, part of it is taking the time to really be the chess master that you talked about. This is going to require you to not only hear these ideas, but actually put them into place.

If you listen to our podcast on a weekly basis, just taking one thing from it and doing one thing new every week, or adding one thing to our already existing strategy and marketing plan and marketing process, is just going to continue to make it better.

But it is consistency. You have to really continually keep looking at it, because marketing is really psychology – applied in a certain way – and math. It's behavioral psychology and math, and that's what produces profits and results as you apply it to a business.

# Episode 105
# The One About Even More Email Marketing

Dean: Hey, everybody. It's Dean Jackson.

Joe: And me, Joe Polish.

Dean: And, me. So, how was 25K?

Joe: It was good. I am really tired, right now, and I just want everyone listening to know that I, with my dedication to doing this podcast and making sure that everybody continues to get all of this stuff, I crawled myself out of bed. It's in the morning, when this is being recorded, and I'm tired, because we had a 2-day 25K meeting. Prior to that, I had 2 days of meetings. I can't even remember what it was.

Dean: Secret meetings?

Joe: What's that? Secret meetings? Yes.

Dean: Secret meetings? It's inflection. It's the way you say it.

Joe: Well, you can inflect for me. I'm just going to talk.

Dean: That's what I'm saying. That's why I added the inflection, because you said you were very forthcoming about what the last 2 days was about, 25K. And then you said, "Before that, 2 days of meetings," which is very mysterious. That's why I said, "Secret meetings?"

Joe: Well, one of them was meeting with Dan Sullivan for like half the day, about our new podcast, the 10X Talk, and then Stefan, who has a company called MagicFuture.com, which is really cool. Magic Future. It used to be Magic Number. The main brand is Magic Future, although they still have Magic Number. It's about finding that number that is what you need to be financially free, so that work is optional.

        Although, I can't imagine ever not working, because

all the money in the world, I would still work on things. Part of, I think, being fulfilled, at least for me, is producing more than I consume. I just couldn't imagine sitting around, whatever, people's idea of, "What would you do in retirement?" "Oh, I'd sit on the beach and read," or whatever. I'm getting ready to sit on the beach.

Dean: Play shuffleboard, be the shuffleboard champion. We'd be doing shuffleboard info products.

Joe: Maybe. I've never played shuffleboard. Have you? Have you played shuffleboard?

Dean: Well, I live in Florida, which is probably the shuffleboard capital of the world. So, I'm not going to sit here and say that I have not ever played shuffleboard, because I have. I don't seek it out. I'm not in a league or anything.

Joe: Let me reveal something that shows you how human beings are kind of strange, including the one talking right now.

I live in Arizona. I've lived in Arizona for many, many years – probably at least 30, 35 years of my life. Maybe 30 years. I've never been to the Grand Canyon.

Dean: And I've been to the Grand Canyon. Isn't that something?

Joe: Yeah. I go to Sedona all the time. Another hour, hour and a half, there's the Grand Canyon. I don't go. But I'm going to go, this year. I'm going to go to the Grand Canyon, because I just realized how idiotic that is.

Dean: Let's go do an episode sitting on the ledge of the Grand Canyon.

Joe: I've done the Galapagos, I've been to Vietnam, and I've been to Australia and New Zealand. I've been to Paris. I've been to England. I've been to Bali. I've never been to the Grand Canyon. I've been to Toronto, even, many times.

Dean: Many, many times.

Joe: So, basically, what I was saying was we're going to talk about email marketing. This is a follow-up of the last episode that we did. I think the last thing that we said, on the last episode, was, "Start off with the email 'Do you want to be on Oprah?'"

Now, I always think it's kind of funny where people that have never been on Oprah, and neither Dean nor I have been on Oprah – although I've met Oprah twice. I actually spent a little bit of time talking with her the very first time she went to Maryville Spa, a decade ago, or whenever that was, when I ran into her there. The spa director, at the time, was giving us a tour, and she was my friend, but she couldn't mention who the VIP's were. We just happened to run right into Oprah, and I suggested that Oprah do the equine experience that they do there, which was kind of cool at the time.

A great spa. I loved that place for many years, and then the general manager, I thought, was kind of a goofball. I think he's the current one. Anyway, I haven't been to Maryville since. Although, Steve Case now owns it. It's a nice resort.

Anyway, that being said, then I ran into her in 2006, at the Oscars, the one and only time I went to the Oscars. But I've never been on Oprah.

However, it's always good, the Oprah link. A lot of people use it. Start off with an email, "Do you want to be on Oprah?"

So, those are my notes. We're going to do that with email marketing. And, like I mentioned, I'm tired. I went to dinner with Dan Sullivan and a few other people, and Brian Kurtz was having dinner with Hugh Downs. Remember Hugh Downs?

Dean: I do remember Hugh Downs, yeah.

Joe: Hugh and his wife have been married 69 years. He's 92 years old, and I think she's 91. I interviewed him on video, for Genius Network, when he was 87. It was a great interview. I'm telling you, man, I talked with him for a few minutes, last night. Just incredibly sharp. Remembers everything. Had the world record for most amount of time on broadcast television. Just an amazing human being.

So, anyway, I woke up early to do this podcast, so people are probably sick of listening to me babble.

Dean: You woke up so early, that you actually woke me up.

Joe: Yeah, and you're 2 hours ahead of me.

Dean: I know.

Joe: So, let's hit it. Let's talk about some valuable email marketing stuff, and maybe I'll touch on some things that we talked about at 25K, if I can get my brain to remember those, too.

Dean: So, last time, we talked about this idea of using the 9-word email, of using just short, personal, expecting-a-reply emails, knowing that the only purpose of the email is to get a response. You've got to know what it is that you want somebody to do, when they read your email. What's the purpose of it? Is it just to deliver information? That's fine. It doesn't really matter how you do that. Send that out.

But when you want a response, you've got to realize and understand what the response is.

We mentioned that the 2 most likely responses are to either reply to this email or click on this link. That's really the bottom line. That's what we're trying to get somebody to do, to take an action.

Both of those are great. The thing about getting a reply is that you can now engage in a dialogue with people, and there are so many, many ways to use this. We'll talk about some of those, because it really is about being and thinking like a chess master, where you've got the ability to kind of guide a conversation with people. You can go hrough the process of having a conversation just like if ou were standing in line at Starbucks with them. You could have the conversation be a very valuable interaction, one person to another person, rather than just using email as a broadcasting tool.

The difference between walking into Starbucks and getting up on top of a chair and saying, "Excuse me, everybody! Can I have your attention for a second, please?" and then sharing your information with everybody. That's like a broadcast. And the difference would be quietly going into line and just striking up a conversation with one person, while you're looking them right in the eyes.

That's the most effective thing that you can do. That's the most responsive thing, because you're...

Joe: Wait! Let me ask you a question, though. I agree with you. I'm just going to play devil's advocate here.

Let's say that someone had a message that did need to be broadcast. Like, "Attention, everybody! The place is on fire. Get out now!"

Dean: Right. Exactly. There you go. That's exactly it: knowing what your purpose is. Sometimes, the purpose is to broadcast information, and there's nothing wrong with that.

But when you're trying to get a response, when you're trying to maximize the engagement that you can with the people on your list, the people who have their email address or the people who have opted in, when you're trying to get the maximum engagement with them, speaking to them one person at a time is the most effective thing you can do.

Joe: What sort of stories or examples do you have to validate this, other than the hundreds that we've talked about in the past, on past episodes?

Dean: I know. There are so many different ways. I'm going to talk about some of the during unit things today, too, a little bit later.

As far as the 9-word emails go, or the engaging emails, or thinking through the process, it's so powerful to really realize that your purpose in the before unit is to generate and convert leads into appointments or sales or first-time purchases, or engagements. You're moving people all the way through the 8 profit activators.

When we talk about your target market, select a single target audience, you've got the people that you already have an email with. You're going to compel them to raise their hand: "Joe, are you still looking for a house in Winter Haven?"

Now, when he's engaged, now we're going to engage in that conversation, and we're going to educate and motivate him to join us for a daily tour of homes or to come to our homebuyer workshop, or to get a free home loan report, whatever it is that you're most interested in. What would be the most effective thing for you, right now? What would be the most valuable thing for you? We're moving people in that direction. That's really what I'm talking about here.

So, when we look at the types of email addresses that you're likely to have, you are likely to have an email address from somebody who has just opted in moments ago, or you are likely to have an email address that you've had in your list for 60, 90, 120 days, 2 years. You're likely to have people who've never bought anything from you; they've opted-in in the past. That's kind of the spectrum of emails that you are likely to have, somewhere on that scale. They've either just opted in, or they've been in for more than 90 days.

Why that's important is because we need to understand, first, the dynamics of what happens when people come into your email, their buying cycle. How long is it between the time that they opt-in and the time that they actually buy?

So, if you're doing things that are sort of early lead generation things, things where you are offering something, like to our lakefront homeowners, the report on lakefront house prices. You're going to generate people who are going to be interested in that information now, but they may not actually sell their lakefront house for 90 days or 6 months, or a year from now. And there may be situations where somebody's going to opt-in, and then they may buy right away.

But you need to understand that and you need to have a sense of what the cycle is in your business. What is the cycle in how long it's going to be before somebody actually buys?

When we talk about converting leads, when I really started going deep into understanding lead management and lead conversion, this was one of the things that was really went in depth on, was the timeline of things.

I don't know whether I've talked about it, but there's a company called The Inquiry Handling Service, and they are a company that if you've ever seen at tradeshows or in trade publications or magazines, where you circle the reader service card, the business reply request, and you send it in and they'll send you information about something. So, if you're looking through a home decorating magazine and you were interested in these faucets, you can circle that on the reader card and send it in, and they'll pass that on to the company, to send you information about the faucets, or same thing at a tradeshow.

So, these guys handle millions of leads across all kinds of different industries. And what they found, by doing an analysis of when people buy, was they were able to identify sort of across-the-board patterns.

The way they would get this data is they would do what they called "Did you buy" surveys. If you inquired about surveys, they would call you up at 90 days and they'd say, "Hey, Joe, you inquired about faucets a few months ago. Have you bought faucets yet?" And you would say yes or no.

And then, they would follow up again, in 6 months or 9 months, 12 months. They follow up with a sampling of people all the way across, for 18 months. And what they found was that just over half of the people who inquired about something will buy what it is they've inquired about within 18 months.

So, there's a good chance, a 50% chance that somebody inquiring about anything is actually going to buy it in the next 18 months.

Now, what they also found was that only 15% of them were going to buy in the first 90 days. So, that means 85% of the value of a bundle of 100 leads, let's say, is 90 days or longer out. They're more than 90 days away from buying.

Now, most of the time, people are largely impatient with the leads. They want to kind of squeeze the most they can out of the leads right away. And if they don't buy right away, then they often get discouraged and think, "Those leads are no good. They were unqualified, or they're just lookie-lou's, or they're not going to buy."

You see this happening all the time with people who do opt-in marketing. They'll send people to a squeeze page. They'll get their name and email, and then they'll blast them for 7 or 10 or 14 days in a row, trying to get as many of them to buy as they can, right now. And then, that's their follow-up cycle, and then they just drop them off a cliff. They don't have any sort of concerted effort.

They only count their conversions on that little window. They only take it on how good people converted right on the front, not realizing that the majority of the value is longer than that.

So, when we look at it, you look at the value in realizing that there's a lot of those people who are going to buy later, and setting up your system so that you can continuously add value to those people, where you can continuously be in communication with them, that's where we'll talk about using a broadcast type of email.

But let's focus on – and where this 9-word email comes from – where this whole idea of engaging with people is let's focus immediately on this first 90 days. This is the group that we want to focus on, because when somebody first ops in, the only person who is going to be monetarily valuable to you right this minute is one of those 15%. If you look at it that if we were to say, "Where should you place your bet?" kind of thing, knowing that 85% of the people are not going to buy right now and that 15% of them are going to buy in the first 90 days. Even 90 days is longer than most people have the patience to follow-up with anybody anyway.

You've seen this all the time. People say, "Let me show you my conversion sequence," and it's like a 7-day sequence, and then it ends. You never really see anybody who's got that kind of concerted follow-up effort beyond those 90 days.

Joe: Let me tell you something from way back when.

I have, in my course for professional cleaners and restorers, which I've sold since 1994, 1995 was when I started selling it to cleaners, and we've had over 7,000 professional cleaners all over the world that have become members and gotten that course, and that sort of thing, one of the letters in there is a 3-step letter for new prospects.

When I first started doing this, there was no Internet, so they were literally printing and mailing them, or putting them in envelopes, or rubber bands, or whatever, and literally placing them, having them hand-delivered to neighborhoods. It was a 3-step letter offering a free room of carpet cleaning and a carpet audit, which is a process that I came up with, which was an educational method to go into a home and evaluate the condition of the carpet. It's a really good offer.

And as it relates to what you're talking about here, the way that I describe it is letter #1, then 2 weeks later everyone that didn't respond would get letter #2, and 2 weeks after that, letter #3.

Very much, a 3-step letter methodology that Dan Kennedy was preaching and teaching, and still does. And that's when I was doing a lot of work with Dan, and he was writing a lot of my sales copy and we were doing a lot of stuff together, and all that. So, we did that for many years.

What we would always tell people is the time to quit going back to the well is when you dip the bucket down and no water comes back. Then, you quit doing it.

So, talking about the length, 90 days, where you're saying people would show a 7-day conversion thing, I just want to point out that the highest number I'd ever seen, one of my clients, a guy named Kevin. I can't remember his last name, right now. This was years ago. I have literally hundreds of people that, even to this day, still use that same letter, same promotion, and it's the basis of many of these companies' new lead generation business.

He had literally taken that same letter to a particular neighborhood and delivered it, every 2 weeks, for 23 different times; meaning he had literally put that letter out 23 times, with just slight changes to the intro of it, before the arithmetic quit working, meaning it was profitable.

I've had many people that have emailed a simple letter 5 times, 6 times, 7 times, and then it kind of grows tired. But he really did his math and calculated it, and built up a pretty successful business with it. And then, he sold the company. That's why I don't remember him, because he built up a company and then he sold it and went and did other things. That was a long time ago.

But we would always say, "You know, people just don't realize that lifetime value of a client and all of the things that we teach, if you want to be in the relationship business, you need to prepare yourself to educate and nurture and do all this stuff that you're talking about here in the context of email."

Dean: Yeah. That's the thing. Even when people set up their sequence, after the opt-in sequence, they're writing it with a tone that is a broadcast tone, that they're still sending it to and communicating it to a group of people. They're not doing it in a way that is a personal interaction.

One of the things that really helps is if you can imagine, just visualize, and I often do this. It's so crazy. You've seen my evil scheme hatchery and the way I have a room up in the front that's got these 2 comfy club chairs with an ottoman. And sometimes, I'll just sit there and I will close my eyes and I'll imagine having a conversation with people. I'll imagine when somebody opts-in, I'll imagine that they're walking into a room and I'm sitting there, right there in the room, and I'm visualizing them. And I'm imagining what would that conversation be like? What would I say to them if I were there with them in person? And that's literally where, if somebody walks in and they're a realtor, they'll opt into our real estate site, that was the exercise that got the conversational email of, "Hey Joe, are you an investor or are you looking for a house to live in?"

So much of that is imagining almost like a personal, real interaction. That's going to help you identify what are the things that are on that person's mind. What do you think they're expecting when they come through? And imagine what if, magically, when they did opt-in, they could be transported into this room? What would they be looking for? What are they expecting to see on the other side of this opt-in? What are they expecting is going to be there? What's the treasure on the other side of that doorway that they're looking for?

Joe: And what is that treasure?

| | |
|---|---|
| Dean: | It's their selfish desires. That's the treasure. It's their selfish desires. It's not about you. It's never about you. It's always about what are they looking for?

So, hopefully, you can be congruent all the way through. When we look at narrowing your focus to a single target market, you've already gone a lot of the way down that path because in profit activator #2, when you offer them a cookie, you offer them something compelling that is going to get them to identify themselves. You know what it is.

I've chosen lakefront homeowners. I've offered them the free report on lakefront house prices. When they opt-in, what is it that they're looking for?

We do the same thing with the buyers. We offer the Guide to Winter Haven Real Estate Prices. And they opt-in. |
| Joe: | I think we should kind of take a retreat back for a couple of episodes back, where we talked about "Branding = Bullshit?" Why not just send out an HTML logo, going back to carpet cleaners, where it's just "Your secret desires are here," with a flower, maybe. |
| Dean: | I like it. |
| Joe: | Or something that would obviously speak to your brand. I'm being sarcastic here, as I say that. Or, "We don't cut corners, we clean them!" |
| Dean: | Right. Exactly. That's funny, because that's one of probably the go-to taglines for carpet cleaners. |
| Joe: | Yeah, one of them. |
| Dean: | Same thing like realtors, "Call Dean and start packing." |
| Joe: | Yeah. Yeah, "25-hour service. We're just a little bit better." |
| Dean: | "Dean Jackson, a house-sold name." |

Joe: Oh, that's funny! That is funny. I like that one. I wonder how many realtors have actually snagged that one.

Dean: Oh, yeah. They're on it all the time.

Joe: The whole thing here is it's not like people want to do ineffective marketing or advertising, they just don't know any better. Unless they're aware of ILoveMarketing.com, which teaches them how to fix all of this bullshit, they're just trying to make a living. They're trying to go out there and sell stuff.

Part of this is taking the obvious and making it happen. Going back to the brand thing, because it's stirred up so many conversations, even at 25K, I read the article and we talked about it. Everyone in 25K is, obviously, of the belief that, "Yeah."

And there are people that have very successful brand that are in 25K.

The point is – you made this comment – it's about them. It's really about their secret desires. So much of people that do brand marketing and advertising, they think they're talking about that, but they're really not using copy that's saying that. They're not using calls to action.

For small business owners, if you spend years and really develop a reputation, I always like to pulling it back to Victoria's Secret, because I did that interview episode #94 with Jeff Madoff, where he talks about Victoria's Secrets being an aspirational brand. Yeah, but that didn't happen overnight, and it certainly didn't happen from a business card or a postcard or a website. There's billions of dollars put into what it is now. You know what I mean?

Anyway, most small business owners, that's not their company. That's not their business. That's not what they're going to be doing.

That's all I've got to say about that. Did you leave the building for a minute or something? What's going on?

Really? Oh, good. You didn't miss anything. I was just babbling about branding. I'm sitting here, thinking I'm talking to you and you're hearing what I'm saying, and all of a sudden...

For people listening to this episode, continue on with your fancy little... Yeah, go for it.

Dean: And, begin.

Joe: When it comes to putting together a plan, I want to frame this. You talked about 90 days. Let's just apply this to every form. How do you think about implementing or engaging a marketing campaign, instead of it just being an email? We're talking about just one part of a full, encompassing plan of communication, lead generation, follow-up, nurturing, etc.

So, when you hear people say things like, "A marketing plan," do you think year out, 90 days, 7 days?

Dean: Here's where it starts. Let's go with this. I think at the very beginning, the only thing that you should focus on, the thing that you really want to imagine is that the person who has just opted-in is a 5-star prospect and is going to buy imminently. That's the best course of action that you can take; not trying to convince them to buy, not try and convince the people who are not that to buy, but to focus only on being there and speaking in a way that would let the people who are those 5-star prospects, who do want to buy know that you're here, and you're ready to help them, and here's what I suggest you do if you are ready to buy.

So, when we look at it that when somebody opts-in, you've got to know that they have never liked you more than the moment they press submit on that opt-in page. That's the peak of your relationship.

Now, what happens from there is either going to continue that and amplify it, or it's going to filter it. You're going to either fall out of favor or you're going to endear yourself to them, immediately.

So, when we look at it, we know that and often draw a quadrant with this. So, if you can imagine 4 quadrants and the axis, the X- and Y-axis divided at the top 2 quadrants and the bottom 2 quadrants by "yes, they're going to buy," or "no, they're not going to buy." And then, the left and right divided into "now" or "later." We'll call later 90 days or more from now.

So, if we go clockwise from the upper left, we'll call that quadrant one, it's "Yes, they're going to buy, and they're going to buy now." We'll call that 90 days. That means according to all those studies, 15% of the people fall into quadrant one.

If we look at all that research and we know that 90 days or more is one of the options, 85% of the people fall into that quadrant 2.

And then if we go down on the bottom, it doesn't matter whether they fall into either of those quadrants, because they're part of the 50% that are not going to buy.

So, there's nobody that matters below the line. All we're worried about are the 50% of the people at the top, who are going to buy, and whether they're going to buy now or whether they're going to buy later.

So, our first strategy has to be focused on that 15%, because, in reality, it doesn't matter what you do to the 85% until 90 days from now, because they're not going to buy for 90 days anyway. Right?

So, the only people that we can speak to, that are going to have value or desire to actually do something today, are the 15% who are in quadrant one.

Now, what we look for there is we're looking for 5-star prospects. We're looking for people who meet some basic criteria. So, I'll share what we look for on the real estate side. And this applies basically everywhere.

We look for people who are willing to engage in a dialogue. That means that when you send them an email, they'll respond. They reply to you. They're friendly and cooperative when they talk with you. They know what they want, meaning the top 15%, the ones who are going to buy now, they know what they want and they're willing to share with you what it is. They've got a plan.

Number 4 is that they're going to buy in the next 90 days. They're now prospects. That would be a 5-star prospect.

And then #5 is that they'd like you to help them.

So, anybody who meets those 5 requirements is a 5-star prospect. And the only thing we're trying to do initially is identify who those 5-star prospects are. And there's no way to do that, unless you start at the top and see who is willing to engage in a dialogue, because that's the first step.

So, that's why when we send out simple emails, we'll give them a chance to first tell us more information, identify themselves. Somebody coming to the real estate site, they leave their name and their email.

Whenever I talk about lead conversion, I talk about lead statistics, all these kinds of things, it always makes more sense of these numbers if you think in terms of a bundle of 100 people. You can wrap your mind around that. You can figure out what the value is of those, and how these numbers make sense.

So, if we take 100 opt-ins and we were just to personify them and line them up, you've got 100 individuals standing there in a line, there's no way, just by looking at them, to tell who's who. We know that half of them are not going to buy, so we can eliminate half of them. But we don't know which half. We know that 15 of them are going to buy in the next 90 days.

But, again, just eyeballing them, you have no idea who is among those 15. So, your first job is to separate out the 15 who are going to buy now. How do we do that? We're looking for 5-star prospects, and the first element of a 5-star prospect is that they're willing to engage in a dialogue. So, what do we do? We try and engage them in a dialogue.

Now, when you look at that, it helps so much to imagine exactly what I'm describing to you. Imagine that these are real people that you're looking at them, you're looking eye-to-eye with them in your imagination, and what would you really say to them? That's often a barometer of whether the email that you're about to send is going to make sense. If you imagine reading it one person to one person, often it will identify itself as a broadcast email or something that you wouldn't actually say to somebody.

Joe: Right.

Dean: What do you think about this so far? Give me your summary. I want to hear what you're hearing.

Joe: What I'm hearing is that placing a real emphasis on communicating in ways that people understand simply, that really speaks to them, doesn't over-complicate anything, talks to people with the right message at the right time, and delivers no more than what they need but exactly as much as they do need in order to step them through the process of doing business with you.

When I listen to this, I really listen for the psychology behind it, not the technology. You're not really talking about, "Here's the email system you should use." It's none of that.

Now, to a certain degree, if someone really is hung up on that and they really don't know where to go, then they may be like, "Wow! How do you do this?"

I'll mention one thing. Dean Graziosi, he was in

25K. He stopped by 25K yesterday, and he was talking about how his current social community at DeanGraziosi.com has thousands of people who will watch, every time he puts up a video, weekly, he'll get thousands of views and anywhere from 300 to 1,000 comments weekly, from these videos he'll put up there, and how engaged the community is.

He said before they did that, they were looking at all kinds of different systems. Phoenix College, I think it was Phoenix College he was talking about, they were talking to the people who had built their system and how it had cost millions of dollars to build this customized system. And he said, "You know, I could engage with people more with a yellow pad, writing down the amount of money they spent on this system, because it's really about communicating with the people and getting them to feel and understand."

So, as it relates to everything that you're talking about, there are people that really think, "Well, what's the technology, though? How am I going to deliver this? This sounds all good and everything, but I don't have that sort of system."

The thing, first, is make sure you're selling what people want, not what you think they need, not the technology that you think is the system, but what do people really want?

Your whole thing about striking up a conversation with someone at Starbucks, one-on-one, once you have developed the ability to know how to establish rapport, maintain rapport, develop and nurture, and continue a relationship with one, you can do it to 2. You can do it to 10. You can do it to 100. You can do it to 1,000.

That's kind of what I'm hearing.

I just always go back to the thing that Steve Jobs said at the Worldwide Developers Conference in 1997, where he said, "Start first with the psychology, and then figure out the technology."

Dean: That's brilliant, but that's absolutely true. That's exactly what we're talking about here. Start with that. Know where you're headed.

In the last episode, we talked about that idea of thinking like a chess master and knowing where it's going, knowing where you're ultimately going to lead them once you know what the appropriate place is. That's why #5 in our 5-star prospects is willing to engage in a dialogue, friendly and cooperative, know what they want, moving in the next 90 days, or whatever, doing something, whatever it is you say in the next 90 days, and they would like us to help them.

So, until and unless you know all those first 4, you can't make a prescription for what to do in #5. If you have that kind of engagement with somebody, and they identify themselves through a sorting question, as an investor or as somebody looking for a house to live in, now you can move kind of down that path.

We've done this in so many different ways, asking somebody whether they're looking to lose fat or gain muscle, and go down a different path with those people. Those kinds of things are very valuable as you kind of move. So, you can intelligently have a conversation, but use technology to do it. Use technology to help you automate the process whenever possible.

Joe: Yeah, totally. Touch on email subject lines, again. We've done this many times, but let's go back to that. I'm really going to try to take this to a whole basic level.

I think a lot of people, even quickly, when they're responding to BCC, we talked about, on the last episode, how I sent an email to Richard Branson about Jay Leno, and I think I put in the subject line – I should pull up that email – "Want to be on Jay Leno?" or something like that. It's obvious.

But even the simple thing of someone's name, or "Hey!"

|        | Let's break that down again, because I think it's good if someone hasn't listened to the past episode we did. |
|--------|---|
| Dean:  | The main job of the subject line, the only job of the subject line is to get them to open the email. That's the only thing. |
|        | With that in mind, knowing and imagining that they were a wizard... |
| Joe:   | I think Dean has left the building again here. He was right in the middle of mid-speech. So, in case you're listening to this episode and we decide to keep this part in, which we probably will, then you'll at least know what the hell's going on. We'll see, when Dean comes back on, if he can jump right back into what he was saying before, or if I have to cue him. |
|        | So, let's just give it a moment here, and see what happens, because this should be fun. |
|        | While we're waiting, I'm staring at the wall, looking at some artwork that I got from Hugh MacCleod, who has a really freaking cool blog and website called GapingVoid.com. I bought a whole bunch of artwork. Hugh's written a couple of cool books. One's called *Ignore Everybody*, his first one. The second one is called *Evil Plans*, and his third is *Blogging In Your Underwear*. |
| Dean:  | Quit hanging up on me. |
| Joe:   | I've just been talking. By the way, I'm in the middle of something, so let me finish my thought, because I know you went away, so I just started to talk about Hugh MacLeod, how I'm staring at the wall, looking at paintings. You disappeared, and I said, "Let's see if Dean can just pop back into what he was talking about, since he disappeared again." |
|        | So, everything you can leave in, because I'm prepared for these things, Dean. |
| Dean:  | You really are. |

Joe: Talking about Hugh MacLeod artwork, and I've got some on the wall. Hugh started drawing art on business cards. I like the stuff. So, one of them says, "Find something you love to do, and then excel at it." Another is, "Lots of ideas clustering around to form a single working business model," which really speaks to what we talk about at I Love Marketing. We're always talking about different ideas clustering around.

Another one is, "Where can the smallest change make the biggest difference?" I think one of the things that speaks to I Love Marketing is that we're always talking about little things, but if they're implemented and applied they make the biggest difference.

Another one that I've got here is, "The best way to get approval is to not need it."

And then another is, "We do what we do because souls need to be touched."

And then the last one I'll mention is, "Welcome to nobody cares, population 6-billion."

These all have artwork on them. So, without seeing it, it's probably not as compelling as actually looking and seeing the pieces. They do do a customized one.

Dean: Why don't you take a picture with your iPhone and send it to me.

Joe: Yeah, I can. Actually, I will.

There's one that says, "After the big boys fuck it up completely, feel free to give us a call. Piranha Marketing."

Dean: Love it.

Joe: Anyway, can you remember what the hell you were saying?

Dean: I was talking about subject lines and how I tell people to imagine that they're a powerful wizard, and that they can just command people to do something and they'll do it.

If that were the case, then all they would have to put is, "Open this email."

Joe: By the way, I think on my voice, if it disappeared, when I was reading the artwork I think I was not pointing my mouth at the microphone. So, I apologize about that, if I got a little quiet.

Dean: So, beginning with that in mind, that's what we really want the email subject line to say, is, "Open this email." That's the command that we have for it.

So, what are the things that are going to get me to open that? And certainly, if it seems like a personal email from me, that's why you've seen even President Obama, you saw all those that said, "Hey," or my personal favorite is their first name or just those kinds of things, something that is relevant or something that is an RE to something that you've already sent them or that they've sent you. Those kinds of things are getting you in the right direction. And, let's be honest, the subject line on its own, if somebody doesn't want to read it or isn't at least familiar with who or why you're getting this, you can trick people into reading your email, but that's not what we're looking for. You want it to be relevant, and you want them to feel like it's relevant. You want them to feel like there's this sense of welcoming for the email, rather than a jaded sense of, "Oh, I'm opening this, but I know it's a scam," that kind of thing.

Sometimes, you can trick people into reading something, but that's not at all what we're talking about. We want it to be a welcomed thing.

Joe: Do you think this is really hard for most people to get and do this? Or, do you think people just don't focus on things that are really the big lever movers?

Dean: I think it's hard for people. What I think is hard for people is that they have a very hard time being patient and knowing that they'll have more luck taking 3 moves to get somebody to a buying position than they will getting them to buy in one.

And, often, that's the thing, is that people are too impatient. They try and get people to buy right away. That's their focus. They're trying to just get them to buy now.

Joe: Let's address the thing that would cause that, though, because the underlying issue is maybe they're just desperate. They need money. They need to make a sale.

It's kind of like if you want a date, if you're so desperate and you so badly want someone that you literally approach them and creep them out, or the positioning or the status or whatever, is just completely wrong, you just seem weak, you seem uninterested, it's the dilemma that I think many guys who are genuinely true, nice human beings – or at least they think the nice things, sometimes they disguise not being nice at all with being nice – they can't get a date because they appear extraordinarily desperate or needy, and that becomes unattractive to someone.

Well, I think your prospects respond the same way. If your whole approach is you so badly want to make a sale, they see right through that.

Part of your think talking about patience, I think it's a really important issue. However, until we eliminate the danger of, "I really badly need money"…

You remember that black velvet poster? People in other parts of the world won't probably know this store, but there's that store Spencer's, which sells gifts and has been around for years.

Dean: Yeah.

Joe: You can find this online, if you search Buzzard or Vulture or whatever, "Patience," where there's 2 buzzards sitting on a branch, and there's like a skeleton of a cow. I've seen different versions of this drawing. One buzzard has got a little thing above his head. I think we've talked about this before. I'm so damned tired from finishing 25K last night, I can't even remember if we've talked about this before.

But there's a little thing that says, "Patience, my ass! I'm gonna kill something." They're waiting for something to die, for them to eat, and they're starving. So, one of the vultures is like, "Patience, my ass! I'm gonna kill something," as he's saying to the other one. But, a lot of people that are in that situation, where they just so badly want it, that they're making decisions that they think are needed, but it's undermining their ability to have success. And this happens with marketing.

I always use the analogy "selling is like seduction." You just don't immediately go and approach someone and say, "I want to sleep with you." It's going to creep them out.

You have to develop rapport. You need to do those things.

So, if someone's in that catch-22 situation where they need a sale today to pay their rent, what do they do?

What I always say is, "If you're really in that situation and you don't have any money to do any marketing, you don't have any time, you're going to have to have time, because if you don't have money, the only thing you've got is time and resources. And if you don't have resources, you have to be resourceful. Literally, go out and talk to people one-on-one, if you need to. Although, if you do the stuff we're telling you, you can eliminate that. When I was a dead-broke carpet cleaner, I was literally doing manual labor. But I had to do that until I could establish even a little bit of foundation to create a marketing system. But you've got to put in the wood in order to get the fire sort of thing.

So, I just want to really speak to that person in that

situation, because I think they can hear what we're saying, but the desperate need to get their business working or they might be on the brink of financial collapse.

Dean: Here's what can ease their mind. What can ease their mind is if you imagine those 100 people lined up, again, as your bundle of 100 opt-ins, and knowing that 15 of them are 5-star prospects who are going to buy right now, meaning in the next 90 days, there's nothing you can do to create those people. You're not going to convince somebody. What you're looking for is identifying who those 15 are. That's what's most valuable to you.

Once you know who they are, now you can communicate with them in a way that's going to get them to the end result faster.

So, even though it seems initially like it's delaying, it's not delaying at all. You want to engage. We're trying to move somebody through this 5-star prospect filter as fast as we can. So, we first have to decide. It's almost like the staged lighting system at the drag races. You know how when they've got that tree of lights and the first light comes on, and then the next one and the next one, and then they're off kind of thing, it's the same thing that we're looking for here. We want this to happen as fast as that. And it can happen right away. Are they willing to engage? Are they friendly and cooperative? Yes. Do they know what they want? Yes. Are they ready now? Yes. What would you like them to do? Buy now.

That can happen very quickly. We've had it happen as fast as opting-in today, coming out, looking at a house tomorrow, and buying it. It can happen that fast.

But somebody who's not going to be ready for 6 months from now, no matter what you say, you're not going to convince them to buy on your timetable. What you're trying to do is skillfully identify the people who are ready right now, and make the right offer to them, that's going to get them to take that action now.

Joe: Yeah, totally. We've got just a few minutes left, maybe 3 minutes left, or whatever. So, I would like you to kind of wrap up and kind of summarize what we've talked about, mostly what you've talked about. I'm glad you did this, because although I get totally energized from doing 25K meetings, I just woke up too damned early today, in order to do a podcast episode with you, because I'm getting ready to go, in a week, to Turks and Caicos, so I've got to knock this bad boy out.

Dean: Knock this bad boy out.

Joe: Knock it out. You know what I mean?

Dean: I hear you.

Joe: I know this was thoroughly pleasurable for you, Dean, just to be on the phone here and recording with me, but beyond that, I've got things…

Dean: It really has been quite enjoyable. Delightful.

Joe: So, summarize the stuff that we've talked about.

Dean: Here's where we are. We're not done yet.

Joe: Of course. We have to do this for the rest of our lives, I think.

Dean: I know. People have to be patient.

Here's what I think where we basically are. Knowing that the fundamental thing is realizing who we're actually talking to, right now. We're focused on these people who are in that 90-day window, the ones who are going to buy now. We want to identify those people. We want to engage them in a dialogue. We want to have a prescriptive solution for them that's leading them to taking action, where they're going to do something.

So, that alone, just having that mindset, is really the great foundation for this. And also, realizing that we're going to come back. We're going to circle around, and we're still going to serve these people who are 90 days or more away, because we haven't even talked about them yet.

There are some really powerful ways to communicate with them in a way that you'll be there when it's actually time for them to do something.

So, just be aware of that. Know that this is really about patiently engaging one person at a time. Even though you're doing it with technology to hundreds or thousands of people, you still want the tone to be that you're doing it to one person, and not being surprised when they respond.

The biggest thing that I often see is we'll suggest to somebody that they send a 9-word email that's going to reengage people, and then they get overwhelmed by the amount of response. We just had that with Kathleen, who came to our Breakthrough Blueprint event you and I did in Phoenix. She sent out a 9-word email to 3,000 people, and she's gotten 1,200 replies, and she's just rushing through, trying to figure out what to say. She's getting it all under control now, but it's invigorating, certainly, because most people, when they send something out, they're not used to having that type of response to something.

Joe: Yeah. You know what's also interesting, too, is that the people who seem to really get this, it's not about hearing it; it's about continually investing and learning how to do it.

The thing is go and spend a little bit of money and do some marketing. And if you're already doing it already, of course you are, you wouldn't be listening to I Love Marketing if you're not doing some marketing. But I want to have you do a little bit more, meaning do a little bit of marketing. Do a little bit more marketing, and pretend, everything that you're doing right now, forget about all that. You're just going to do a little bit more, and you're going to add a little bit more on top of it. And speed of implementation, as our friend Eben Pagan does a really great job of talking about, is the key to taking an idea and really benefiting from it.

So, wherever you're at right now, with everything you've heard on this episode, listen to the previous episode to this, if you haven't, because it really is kind of the beginning part of this one.

Whatever ideas you have, pick one of them. What is the first action you're going to need to do, and just do it.

People like Kathleen and many of our clients, students, friends that use this, they are making thousands of dollars as a result of just making these little tweaks.

So, like the Hugh MacLeod thing I've got here on the wall, "Where can the smallest change make the biggest difference?" think about that as a result of hearing this episode and go do it. We'll talk to you next week.

Anything else, Dean?

Dean: Amen. Just do it.

Joe: There you go. Just do it. Talk to you guys later.

# Episode 106
# The One About Ridiculously Easy Email Stratagies

Dean: Hey, everybody. It's Dean Jackson.

Joe: And Joe, Joe, Joe, Joe Polish.

Dean: Joe, the world traveler.

Joe: I decided to change my first name to say "Joe" like 3, 4, 5, 6 times, and then my last name.

Dean: Why not? If Prince can change his name to a symbol...

Joe: Right. I can change my name to being Joe multiple times.

Dean: Rock stars are eclectic. We can do whatever we want, something like that.

Joe: That is correct. Alright, so I'm back from this trip I did to Turks and Caicos.

Dean: Nobody cares. Let's get on with it.

Joe: It was lovely, except I got mauled by bugs. No one else seemed to get...

Dean: Why is it that you always get mauled by bugs? You get eaten by bugs on Necker Island. That's your biggest complaint.

Joe: I don't get it. I don't get it. And I've ordered Avon Skin-So-Soft, which everyone tells me to get, which supposedly works for bug bites. And I was covered in Off and having poisonous DEET seeping into my skin, and wearing mosquito-repellant clothing from Exofficio. I can never pronounce it.

Dean: Exofficio, yeah. Exofficio. Yeah, yeah.

Joe: The transcriber's going to probably not spell that right, either. Just everything, and I was still getting eaten by bugs. My girlfriend, she was getting bit too, but they weren't turning into welts like me. And, of course, Brendon Burchard felt horrible, because it was his trip that he invited me on. There were really cool people there, and I actually took the house that Frank Kern was supposed to get, and I think I saved him, his wife and his child from getting mauled by bugs, because I was in this particular house.

Dean: While they were in Hawaii, where there are no bugs.

Joe: Did they end up going to Hawaii?

Dean: They did.

Joe: Well, he had a passport issue. He didn't realize for each isle you need a passport.

Dean: Hawaii's a paradise that's available to all Americans without passports.

Joe: I agree. I love Hawaii. It's awesome. Although, I've only been to Kauai and Maui, so I've never been to the big island. But I always stay with Joe Sugarman whenever I go to Maui, because he's got some really bitching pads up there, and he's a real dear friend of mine. Why not?

Dean: That was very nice of him to give all of our attendees at the I Love Marketing conference their very own Batman credit card.

Joe: Yeah. And Blu-Blocker sunglasses to most.

Dean: And Blu-Blocker sunglasses.

Joe: Yeah. Anyway, we're going to talk about email marketing.

Dean: We've been talking about it.

Joe: I think in this one, I'll just sit back and let you pontificate and talk about things, and I'll throw in a sarcastic comment here and there, and liven it up a little bit.

Dean: That would probably be best for everybody.

Joe: Let's teach some people some good stuff. This is a continuation.

So, let's review what we've been over so far.

Dean: I was just going to say, "Let's review so far, and catch up where we are."

So, we started off this whole series, the last 3 episodes, this is the third of the 3-part series, we started out with you knew that email was going to be a big subject. We could honestly probably do 30 episodes about email.

But here's the big thing, just to kind of catch everybody up. We're talking about it as a before unit strategy here. The things that we've been sharing are things that anybody could do right now. It's one of the – I call it – magic tricks that we can create for people without any cost for them, and generate some revenue for people, generate some money very quickly, just by crafting the right 9-word email.

We gave lots of examples about that, and the original that I started with was just sending a message to real estate prospects who hadn't bought or had been on the list for 90 days or more, just sending a quick message that said, "Hey Joe, are you still looking for a house in Georgetown?" – 9 words, simple, easy to do. And all kinds of people respond, because it feels like you're talking just to them.

So, we talked a lot about this idea of using short, personal, expecting-a-reply emails as a way to engage people in a dialogue. And this is a one-to-one approach. This is definitely not something that you're going to automate. We can automate the initiation of the dialogue, but once somebody raises their hand, once somebody responds to the email, now you've got the best opportunity ever because you have the attention of somebody who's a real person. If you can imagine them as a real person, just like I shared how I do in my evil scheme hatchery, to sit here and visual a prospect, I visualize the front door of my evil scheme hatchery as the opt-in box, and I visualize, as they opt-in, popping through the door and standing there as a real person, not just a name and an email address. But I picture the real person standing there, and I imagine what would I say to that person. What would I say if that real person popped through that door?

That kind of thinking is really the way to get inside your real prospect's mind, kind of the way that you would do it if they really were standing there in front of you. It changes the way that you communicate. Because if you truly are talking to one person, you're going to communicate differently than if you're broadcasting to a group. And people know the difference. And it's okay that sometimes you are broadcasting to a group, and sometimes you're communicating one-on-one. And you want to make sure that the times that you are communicating one-on-one, that people really know that it is meant to be a personal communication.

That's why when we look at it, the pattern that seems to unfold, we'll ask people, "Are you still looking for a house in Georgetown?" and even if they think it's an autoresponder, they will reply with a very short answer because they maybe feel like they might get punked or something. They don't want to look silly responding to a message that is not manned by a real person kind of thing. It's almost like the short responses that you get initially are the email equivalent of somebody turning and saying, "Are you talking to me?"

If you were to say something to them at Starbucks, they might look at you and say that. And then, once they realize that you are talking to them, then you're engaged in a dialogue now. So, we find that if you know where it's going – we talked about sorting questions – if you can ask somebody a question, "Are you looking to lose fat or gain muscle?" that's an either/or option, and you're prepared for whatever the answer is.

Somebody might respond to that initial question with a one-word reply or a very short reply, and that's okay. In this way, by asking a sorting question like that, you know what the 3 possible responses are going to be. The 3 possible responses are: 1) I'm looking to lose fat; 2) I'm looking to gain muscle; or 3) no response at all. Those are the 3 basic options that you're going to get.

You can be prepared for what to say when they respond with either one of those.

And now, when you go back to them, when you're really engaged in that dialogue, you'll find that after a couple of exchanges, they'll know that they're in dialogue with a real person, and they'll send you what I call "the love letter."

The love letter is when they open up and now, because they have the attention of somebody who can help them and seems to be sincerely interested in helping them, they'll share everything about their situation. They'll tell you. They'll be so much more forthcoming, and they may ask a question, and they may be more talkative. Just like when you're in a real conversation, if you have a couple of short interchanges and then somebody's going to go off on a little bit of a tear.

And that's exactly what happens with your email dialogues like that. And all of that is designed with one purpose in mind. This sort of dialogue method is designed to focus all of your attention – initially – on the 5-star prospects who want to buy right now.

We talked about the quadrants. We talked about the 4 quadrants of possibilities for when somebody is going to buy or if somebody's going to buy, and I shared some stats from the Inquiry Handling Service about how just over half of the people who inquire about something will buy what it is they inquired about within 18 months of when they inquire about it.

So, what they also found was that only 15% of them would do it in the first 90 days. So, that means that 85% of the value of a bundle of leads, when we talked about separating your leads into bundles of 100 and thinking about them as that sort of class or statistical grouping, so you've got enough people to see what can happen.

After 100 people, typically, what happens with the first 100 will happen with the second 100, and so on.

So, knowing that if you've got 100 people, we divided them into quadrants. There are only 4 possible options. So, on the up-and-down, the top and bottom axis, we put "Going to buy" or "Not going to buy." Those are the 2 options for this group, as a whole. So, we're going to separate the people who aren't going to buy into let's just call it half, because they say just over half are going to buy. But let's just call it half. Half of them are not going to buy. We've got 50 people below the line, that aren't going to matter to us right now, because they're not going to buy now and they're not going to buy later. So, that's okay.

Above the line, we've got the 50 people who are going to buy, and now we can divide those into 2 groups on the left and the right axis. And that would be now or later.

So, the only people that we're focused, and we want to focus all of our attention on the people who are going to buy, and that means that they're going to buy now or they're going to buy later, and we know that 15% of them are going to buy in the first 90 days, and 85% of them are going to buy in the longer than 90-day timeframe.

So, all we're trying to do is get an awareness of what we're talking about. And in the first moments of somebody opting in, in the first few days, literally that first period of interactions there, the only thing that we should be focusing on is speaking to the people who are going to buy and are going to buy now. Give them the opportunity.

So, we're going to treat everybody like they're a 5-star prospect, and we talked about 5-star prospects as people who are: 1) willing to engage in a dialogue; 2) friendly and cooperative; 3) know what they want; 4) doing something in the next whatever amount of timeframe is right for you, 90 days, 6 months, whatever it is; and 5) that they'd like us to help them. That's what a 5-star prospect is.

So, we're looking for the 5-star prospects who are going to buy now. And we're going to focus all of our attention on them. There's nothing wrong with treating everybody like they are a 5-star prospect until they show you that they're not, versus treating everybody like they're not a 5-star prospect until they prove that they are.

And that's the approach that most people take. They have this sense that leads are somehow dirty, almost. The questions people ask, "Are they scrubbed leads?" or "Are they qualified leads?" all those kind of things that foreshadow the treatment that people are going to give them, because they're so concerned; they don't want to waste time.

I'm telling you, right now, that the very best thing that you can do is to treat everybody like they are a 5-star prospect, and waste some time on them. Spend some time. Invest some time in them.

What I'm describing to you, these types of email dialogues, it's time-consuming. It's the most effective thing. It's the thing that's going to get you in dialogue with the most people, and find the most 5-star prospects. You're going to convert more of them.

I'm not saying it's easy. I'm saying that it's effective. It's the thing that's going to get you more than anything else. And it's worth doing. It's worth trying to figure out. It's like we always talk about the idea of not letting logistics dictate what you do. Don't let logistics get in the way of really stellar logic.

We want to focus on those people, and we want to engage them in a dialogue. And if you have the ability to staff that role, even if you're doing it in high volume, it could be somebody's whole responsibility. Like an email concierge, an email dialogue generator, somebody who that's their role is to engage in a dialogue. That's what we have with Lillian here, running the websites for Living In Winter Haven. That's her whole role, is to engage with people. And, she's able to connect with more people than anybody else would be able to, because they're trying to fit it in when they've got some time. But it's her whole responsibility.

That's a powerful way to think about it. So, we shared some of the engagement strategies in the last episode. What I want to kind of focus on now is moving into this bigger group of people, that 85% of the people who are not going to buy right now. It pains me to see how much people lose by not having a real, concerted strategy for communicating on a long-term basis, that adds value to all of those people who have raised their hands, knowing that that's really where all the gold is in your list.

It's so funny. I had a client – I won't say who this was – that generates thousands of leads, and they have a high-volume system for finding the people who are going to do something right now. They kind of pride themselves on they've got this 21-day process that they take people through this 21-day follow-up thing, and they're able to convert about 10% of the people who come in through that process. It's a high-dollar thing, so it's a really great conversion process.

But then, their words were that after they go through that 21-day cycle, they'd go into the archive, is what they called it.

I had them set up a swear jar, and I said, "If we refer to that group of people as anything other than the goldmine, from now on, I want people to put $100 in that swear jar. I never want to hear the word 'archive' again."

We were able to craft some simple, simple messages that go to these people, that we're able to bring out hundreds of thousands of dollars of new business, doing this.

You're sitting on a goldmine, if you have been using opt-in email marketing, where you're bringing people to a squeeze page and they leave their name and their email address.

Don't ever let yourself get complacent about that. Don't ever let yourself underestimate the value of that.

When somebody leaves their name and their email address, they now move into your profit activator #3, where we can educate and motivate them.

So, we focus on the first group. We focus on the 15%, the ones who are going to buy right away. And we do that by really engaging in a great dialogue.

Now, parallel to that and thinking long-term, we immediately want to start implementing a strategy that's going to keep us in contact with those people in a valuable way for a long period of time.

I'm not talking about just setting people up on auto-drip, where they get just this sequence of follow-up messages, trying to squeeze more buying opportunities out of them. I'm talking about educating and motivating these people.

So, you want to think, if you can, about having at least a weekly flagship publication that goes out to everybody. It could be as simple as an email. You could do a podcast, like we do, like the I Love Marketing podcast. We're constantly in contact with hundreds of thousands of people every week, by communicating and adding value. These aren't sales messages. This is adding value. We're building a relationship with people.

You can do that same thing. What would be a dream-come-true for your audience? If you think about our audience as business owners, entrepreneurs, coaches, real estate agents, and carpet cleaners, people who want to apply marketing to their business, what would be a dream-come-true for them is to be able to tune in every week and get actionable, cutting edge strategies that they can apply right away. And that's what we're doing. Every single week, we're sharing the best stuff that we know to our audience, and that builds tremendous relationship with people.

So, what would be a dream-come-true for your audience? For the realtors, we send out a weekly market watch email to all of their prospects who are looking for homes, we send out a market watch email with all of the new listings that have come on the market, some short little dialogue that shares the kinds of homes that you've been looking at or showing, the kinds of people that you've been working with, if you're the real estate agent sending this out, then links to all of the new listings.

And then, we always want to lead to the next step. We always want to keep in mind that we want people to take that next step, and we want to make it easy for them by offering them cookies.

We've talked about this idea of offering cookies is taking the initiative. It's so much more powerful than to wait for your prospects to take the initiative. Nobody likes to take the initiative. It's like the story we always use is saying, "If I sat you in the living room and said, "There's lots of stuff in the fridge. If you're hungry or thirsty, go ahead and help yourself," versus coming right up to you with a plate of freshly-baked cookies and saying, "Would you like a cookie?"

See, these kinds of things, this is the way that society works. We're wired to not want to take the initiative. We want to respond. We want people to ask us for help, because then we can jump into action and we can demonstrate how helpful we are and how enthusiastic we are, and how sincere we are in really wanting to help them. But we're scared to death to make offers to people, because they might reject us.

So, what we want to do is make offers that seem like they're already happening. So, if we look at from our real estate standpoint, if you're a buyer looking for a home in Winter Haven, and you are on our market watch newsletter and you get updates every week, with all the new listings, we know that the next step for you is going to be that you might want to go and look at a home. That's one approach that people have. That might be what triggers them into starting the process.

You may want to figure out how much can I afford before I go jumping into looking at homes? So, we've got another group of people that that's the motivator that's going to spur them into action.

And then we've got maybe people who are new to the home buying process, and they don't know what they don't even know, and they may want to get educated about the entire home buying process first.

So, if you take those 3 things, if I describe them, you can imagine that those are certainly conversations that are going on in people's mind. So, if we take the trigger of wanting to go and look at homes, our expectation is that people are going to take the initiative. So we may say something like, "If you ever want to look at homes, please feel free to email me and let me know. I'd be more than happy to do the research, find the homes for you, and show you any home that you want to see." That's kind of like we're saying, "If you want me to bake you some cookies, I'd be happy to. I've got all of the ingredients here."

Nobody would ever impose on somebody to bake them some cookies like that. But if, instead of saying that, I say, "Hey, if you're going to be in town this weekend, we're doing daily tours of homes every day at 10:00 and 1:00. You can join any of the tours. It's a great way to look at homes in any neighborhood and area that you want to see."

That sounds like you've already baked the cookies. It's on the calendar. The schedule is there. The bus is pulling out of the station at 10:00 and 1:00. That's what it sounds like, so it sounds easy. I'm not obligating myself to anything. I'm not imposing on you. I'm just going to jump on the bus. I'm just going to jump on this tour that's already happening.

Or, if we take the person who might want to know about how much they can afford or understand how the financing works, instead of saying to people, "If you have any questions about mortgages or you'd like to get pre-approved for a mortgage, feel free to email me, and I'll be happy to put you in touch with our lender, who will get you pre-approved right away," or we start mandating it to people and start pushing it on them, "Now, you've got to get pre-approved before you go and look at any homes." Again, treating people like they're not 5-star prospects until they prove that they are.

Both of those approaches are very common. And I'm hoping that, as I'm describing this, you're hearing it and translating it into how your situation might be similar. I'm describing it to you in a real estate situation, but I want you to understand the psychology of the passive approach versus the attractive approach.

So, we're not saying, "You've got to get pre-approved," or we're not saying, "If you'd like to get pre-approved, I can certainly help you." We're saying, "What we offer is our free home loan report, where we monitor hundreds of different loan programs around the country, to find the lowest interest rate loans, the lowest monthly payment loans, the lowest down payment loans, and the lowest total cost loans, and we put all of these findings together in our free home loan report. And you can get one just by clicking here." That sounds like it's already done. It sounds like something that is in place.

I'm not imposing on you to do anything. You've made the offer, here it is, and I can just take advantage of this. And the same thing if somebody wants to find out about the home buying process. Instead of saying, "If you have any questions about the home buying process or any questions at all, please feel free to email me. I'm more than happy to answer any questions. We could talk on the phone."

Just trying to passively be suggesting things to people is not the same as saying, "We're holding a home buyer workshop on Tuesday night, at the library, at 6:00 pm." That sounds like it's already going on, like there's a specific offer that I can take advantage of. I'm just going to show up at the library, and I'm going to get my questions answered.

So, there's that kind of thinking. I want you to think about what could you offer to people who are prospects that this is going to trigger them taking the next step, it's going to trigger them moving into profit activator #4, where you can present your unique service offer.

Joe, are you still there? Are you asleep? I just went off on a tangent.

Joe: I was trying to create a world record of how long I cannot say anything. I think we've literally broken the world record on the I Love Marketing podcast.

Dean: I just get so excited about it.

Joe: You just talked and talked and talked, which is fine.

Dean: It's almost like the contest episode, in reverse. Okay, your turn. I've said some new things here. I've articulated things in new ways. But what's your take, so far?

Joe: I don't care. Whatever. How long have I been doing this crap? 20 years now? More than that. Since 1992. It's kind of a "been there, done that" sort of thing.

But for everyone listening, hey, it's brand new for someone who's heard it for the first time.

Dean: There you go.

Joe: No, I'm kidding. Did we ever put up the episode, as a bonus, interview I did with Mary Ellen Tribby?

Dean: I don't believe we did. We should just have Mary Ellen Tribby on.

Joe: Yeah, we're going to have to do that. But I did this great interview with her, a few years ago, and she made this comment where we talked about how we grew up in the direct mail business. And the thing with Internet marketers is I made this comment that they're more promiscuous with their emails because it's free, in their minds, and they don't have to spend money on it. And she made the comment like, "Yeah. And if you start looking at every email you send as if you had to spend 50¢ per email on each one, you'd really think differently about the person who's receiving it; not just from what you're going to make money-wise, but how you're really doing a disservice to the people you're sending it to, if you don't really think about the copy and engaging them."

So, let's just assume people listening, there's a person out there saying, "Yeah, that sounds good, but my clients are different. An HTML email with graphics and all that is just going to work better, although I've heard about this 9-word email thing. But my clients are different." How would you respond to that?

Dean: Well, your clients are people, I'm assuming, and people are the same. We all come standard issue, with the same brains and emotions, and psychological triggers. And that is why we can take a construct like the 8 profit activators and apply it to any business. And we've done it. We've done it with all kinds of businesses, and it all works, because people are people.

Joe: That is true. But what if your clients really are aliens? Would it change?

Dean: Then you just write the emails in Klingon, which is the intergalactic language of direct response. Everybody knows that.

Joe: I was making some goals the other day. This is a total aside. And I was thinking, "I want to create some prime directives for my business." I was like, "Let me look up Wikipedia, what prime directives means, so I can get a clear thing before I create some prime directives of my business." I was doing this on the island. In my life, not just in my business.

And I didn't realize that all of these prime directives things originated with Star Trek. I had no idea that that's where it originated from.

Dean: And then, of course, it originated in the "More cheese, less whiskers" episode. The prime directives of a mouse. Get cheese; avoid cats.

Joe: I didn't realize how much of this goes back to Star Trek, which is another aside. On my zero G flight was Rod Roddenberry. So, on the videos, if you look at some of the videos, his father created the whole Star Trek, and it was Rod floating right by me. It's pretty funny.

This is common sense that isn't very common, because you have to strip away all of these preconceived notions that you think about what people would respond to. And it's so simple and so obvious, that most people don't think about it until they hear you kind of explain it.

Dean: So, I always like to look at the context of things, about why things work or what's the underlying support structure that makes all of this work.

So, I'm sharing stories about 9-word emails and we're giving examples of that, and sharing things about the flagship publication. I'm using the real estate examples there. But if we just strip that all away, what you want to be looking at is what kind of regular communication could you send to your prospects, all the people in profit activator #3, that they would be thrilled to get every week? Is there news that you can react to?

The good thing is that with the real estate, there are constantly new listings that are coming, that you can send to people. There is something very powerful about that, that it's got the content kind of built right in. You just have to have the right framework around it.

Now, when you look at creating something on your own, like making something up, it's more difficult than just responding to something. But, you can start by just making a list of all of the questions that people might have. Or, think about what would they want to know. So, you can just make a list of the top 20 questions that people have. There's almost half a year's worth of weekly emails, just addressing one of those questions as a short little thing.

I get Seth Godin's blog by email, so every day you get a short, little blog. He's not writing big articles he's writing. It takes you a minute or 2 to read, that's it. It's all very insightful. You feel good after having read it.

So, what kinds of things like that could you send to people? If there's anything that is changing, if you're in the mortgage business, we send information on interest rates. The same thing could apply to financial advisors. It could be any kind of data that changes or fluctuates. You can talk about volatility or anything in the stock market. Anything that's moving is a great thing to design your weekly flagship around.

But the most important thing about it is that the purpose of it is that it's like a Trojan horse, in a way. It's the carrier that you can now make these offers every single time you send out a communication. You can make the offer that has whatever your 3 cookies are in a super-signature. A phrase that I coined, that is describing, below the PS of the letter, before all the unsubscribe stuff or almost like a little ride-along with every email that you send, all the offers that you can make to people.

So, "Here are 3 ways we can help you today. Join us for a daily tour of homes. We run tours every day, at 10:00 and 1:00." There's one of those super-signature elements.

"Next, we're holding a first-time homebuyer workshop next Tuesday, at the library, at 6:00 pm." Or, offer, "The free home loan report, where we monitor all the different loan programs and present our findings in the home loan report. Click here."

So, you've got those 3 offers that are available for people right there, no matter what.

Whenever you've got something that's going to trigger the next step, you can include it in your email as a super-signature. And that, you're going to find every time we send out a market watch email, we end up getting more people raising their hand and responding to ask for one of the offers that we make in the newsletter.

I'll put up one of the market watch newsletters on ILoveMarketing.com. So, if you're just listening to the podcast here, there's a good reason to go to ILoveMarketing.com and see what one of these flagship emails looks like, and how you can use that as a model for your business.

Joe: I completely agree with that. They should do that. They should go there immediately, right now.

Dean: I think that's fantastic.

Joe: Let me ask you a question, Dean. All of this with email, and I know we've talked for a week on this stuff, I'm sitting here thinking that someone listening is like, "Okay, you're going to put all this thought and effort into getting an email right. Man, if it's this complicated, what the heck are we supposed to do with our websites? Do we even need a website?" That sort of thing.

Dean: Well, certainly. This is why, when I look at it, in my opinion, the reason that I use such short-copy landing pages, the squeeze page where the only option, the only purpose is to get them to leave their name and email, now I never care if they ever go back to the website, because now I've got their email address. And that's a far more powerful level of communication. Now, I can communicate with them one person at a time. And I don't have to depend on them coming back to the site.

But I know that since I can't count on them to continue coming back to the site, the super-signature is a way of sending the highlights of the site to them every week. It's almost like reminders, "Hey, you can get this. You can get this. You can get this." All really compelling things. Things that are well thought out, the things that people would really appreciate getting, because they're demonstrating that you understand the conversations that are going on in their head.

Joe: Let me ask you about something related to driving people to calls to action, other than just an email response.

Is there any deviation from the 9-word email, where you're going to "Are you interested in losing weight or putting on muscle?" "Do you want your carpets cleaned?" whatever, "Looking to buy a home?" where you actually drive them to a website as part of that?

Dean: Sure. I think I talked about the example of we have a product called GettingListingsSold.com, and we get the data feed of all of the MLS listings that come on the market everywhere in the country. So, we get probably 3,000 to 5,000 listings a night come in.

The whole purpose of that email, and I described it in one of the last episodes, is only to get people to click through to the website. I'm not trying to get them to respond. I'm trying to get them to go and look.

So, we do things like we send out an email with the address of the property that you just listed in the subject line. Remember, the only purpose of the subject line is to get them to open the email.

So, if you just listed 22 Graystone, and you get an email that the subject line is "22 Graystone," you're going to want to see what that's about, because it could be somebody who wants to see it or has a question about it. Right? That's an A-pile email subject line.

Then, when they open it, the only purpose of that message, then, is to get them to click through to the site because we've built all these wonderful things for them using the information that they sent in to the MLS. It's already loaded. We've got postcards with the picture of their new listing, and their picture and their name, and the address of the property. It's already custom designed.

So, all I want them to do is take a look at all this stuff. The email just simply says, "Hi Joe, I put together some marketing ideas for 22 Graystone. Take a look and let me know what you think." And then, there's a blue link to 22 Graystone. "Thanks, Ramona." And that's it. And that email gets over 30% click-through. Not 30% open; 30% of the people click through to that website. That is 10 times better than the previous effort, which was in the 3% range, sending all of the message trying to convince them to buy the postcards from the email.

So, they see what it's about, they know that you're trying to get them to spend money, so they don't click through because they've made up their mind already. You can't use the email to do the best selling job. It's not the right environment.

When I've got beautiful, customized things that they're going to get a wow factor by going to it, when they see a single property website that's already done for them and they see these beautiful postcards, and it's already got the picture of their new listing in it, and they see their name, and all of these things are already done, that's a wow factor. And the headline, it's all personalized for them.

So, that can be best sold when they are actually looking at it, and I can control the environment on the website. Everybody's going to see the same thing. I don't know what is going to happen in somebody's inbox, or depending on what email they're using and whether they've got their HTML display images filter off so that the first thing they'll see is, "To see this email properly, click here." That's a real downer.

But if it's just a text email and the only purpose is just to get them to go to the website, that's all you need to do. You don't have to now make all those other offers, and I don't want them to respond.

But what you do have to know is you have to have absolute clarity on what it is you want them to do. Why are you sending this email in the first place? What's the response that you want?

Joe: Let me ask you about something that is on my mind, currently. I just want to get your perspective on it.

You remember TV shows like Nip Tuck, which maybe you've watched? Remember that TV show?

Dean: I do, yeah.

Joe: About the plastic surgeons, the crazy ones. Eccentric.

Dean: Yep.

Joe: That was like real life, basically. I think that show depicted how life really occurs for most people.

But they used to advertise the hell out of MySpace. They would put MySpace.com/NipTuck, when MySpace was the big rage. Maybe with Justin Timberlake taking it over, maybe it will come back.

I saw a Ford banner in the airport the other day. It was for one of their vehicles, and it was simply driving people to their Facebook page, not to their website.

So, what's interesting about that is they don't have to, obviously, set up a website. They can just drive to Facebook. But there's more and more of that that we're seeing, and I wanted to get your perspective on this sort of application, driving people to other than your own websites, to things like Facebook, or even communicating with 9-word emails in a social media sort of environment, not through just regular email. Do you have any perspective on that?

Dean: I like to send them to environments that I can control. I want to know, because I'm thinking ahead, I'm thinking the next move after this. That's what I want. I'm not only thinking about this move; I'm thinking about where's that going to get them. What is the next thing that they're going to do?

So, I want to take them to the environment that's going to best facilitate that. Using these postcard examples, what I want them to do is buy the postcards. So, I'm going to take them to the page where the buy button is, and make the full case. I'm going to present everything to them right there, and they're going to see it, and they're going to be able to click and buy right now, because that's what I want them to do.

Joe: Okay. What else does someone need to know, then? To take what you've been talking about here and what we've talked about in the last couple of episodes – which, if someone has not listened to them, they'd be well-served to go and do that – what more do they need to know to maybe do some action steps? How would you take all the advice that we've given on the last 3 episodes? What's the first step, sit down, write an email, send it out?

Dean: The first step is if you don't have a list of people who have left their name and email, then you want to back yourself up to profit activator #2, and create a compelling offer that's going to get somebody to leave their name and their email address. That's the first thing that you want to do. And, realize the value, the goldmine that you can build by having an opted-in list of people who have responded to an offer that you've made. That's where you want to start.

Then, you want to start with imagining a real conversation with a real person, if the opt-in box that they've filled in was a portal to your office, where they're going to plop themselves right down in front of you, and you can have a real conversation with them, where you can't ignore them.

You've got to realize that behind every email is a real person. Imagine what's going on in their mind. Imagine that person. Get a crystal clear picture of them in your mind, and try having a conversation with them.

That's why I said it looks crazy, if you were to spy in my office and you see me sitting in my comfy Manhattan club chair with my ottoman and my feet up, staring out my glass front door, imagining a conversation with somebody. It looks like I'm just kind of sitting there, goofing off, but I'm actually really deep into that process of having those conversations with people.

I want to be extra careful that you don't underestimate the effort and the consideration and the weight that I place on every single word of those emails. Just because they're 9-word emails, it's not about just plopping off 9 words. That's not what it's about. Every word has weight. Every word has been measured and really is the best articulation. Even when you're using those short words, you just want to make sure that it's getting the right message across.

So, I may spend an inordinate amount of time writing a 9-word email or writing a short email like the 22 Graystone email, but measuring every word to make sure that it's conveying just the right message, that's going to get exactly the action that I want.

You know what would be a fantastic thing? I'm just thinking as we do this, Joe. What would be a great finale to this is to do sort of an email clinic, where listeners could, in

|       | the comments, put their email ideas, their attempts at the 9-word emails or short emails that they've used for things, and we could do an episode that kind of ties all this together and addresses those, and does some coaching on how to make those emails work. That would be great. |
|-------|---|
| Joe:  | There have been some really great comments, too. I've seen a couple of examples. |
| Dean: | That's what I'm saying. So, let's formalize that. When this episode goes up, as soon as you hear this, go over to ILoveMarketing.com, look for the comments. There's a little button that you can use to comment right underneath where the description of this episode. This is episode one of 6. So, look for it on ILoveMarketing.com. Leave a comment. Describe the scenario of what the email is, what your purpose for it is, and then we'll be able to see what you're doing there, and we'll do an episode where we talk about those emails, and we'll give you some coaching on how to craft those into the most powerful emails that we can imagine. |
| Joe:  | Yes. Another thing, too, that we could do, because we've had a lot of questions submitted in the past whenever we've done the open sort of calls… |
| Dean: | We've still got all of those. You're right. |
| Joe:  | Yeah. We could answer some of those questions, too, in some upcoming episodes. |
| Dean: | It's about time we had a guest, too. We've been going a long time, just me and you. I think Mary Ellen would probably be a very good… This is the appropriate time for that. |
| Joe:  | We're going to have some bonus ones, too. Let's put up the episode with Mary Ellen, and it will be a good primer for everyone. It's just really, really good, solid marketing advice. And I'll round up Mary Ellen, and maybe we'll do one with Larry Winget, who's a good friend and a character. We'll do him sooner or later. We'll see. |

Who else have we got? We've got Ben Altadonna. I want to do one with Ben Altadonna. He's the guy that markets to chiropractors, a very smart direct response guy.

Dean: How about Jay Abraham?

Joe: We can probably do one with Jay. I haven't talked to Jay in about a month or so, so I can give him a call. Yeah. It's all good.

To our listeners, if you have a dream interview you think would be awesome, someone that's truly obtainable and reachable – like I wish we could get Oprah, but that's just not going to happen, plus getting her to talk about marketing.

Can you imagine if we got Oprah talking about marketing, though?

Dean: I don't want to limit the universe.

Joe: Aliens. If anyone has a good connection with an alien.

Dean: Yeah, there we go.

Joe: Then we could talk about packaging, that sort of stuff. That would be good, too.

Dean: Why limit ourselves? We've had Richard Branson. We've had Tony Robbins. Why wouldn't Oprah want to come on with us?

Joe: True. Very true. The New York event is coming up soon, in August, 14th and 15th. So, if you're a high-level player and you listen to this, we've got, so far, people that I will announce, Tim Ferriss is going to be there, Dean Graziosi, Dan Sullivan, Marie Forleo.

Dean: You said Dean Graziosi. I get excited when I hear Dean.

Joe: Neil Strauss. We're going to have some characters there, speaking, doing some cool stuff.

Dean: Yeah.

Joe: So, any good books or anything you've read lately, Dean, that you want to recommend?

Dean: Rather than that, I've got a couple more things I want to say to wrap up this on.

Joe: Okay, go ahead.

Dean: Is that alright with you?

Joe: Fine with me.

Dean: You got me going. I was telling people what to do.

We talked about this idea of crafting that dialogue with people, imagining as if they're a real person, sitting right there, and the opt-in box has plopped them into your office. Have that conversation with them, and then the next thing is to start, right away, with your weekly flagship communication. Every week, they're getting something from you, with timely and helpful market information or answering some of the questions, or tips, or anything like that, or a mailbag, answering questions, anything like that, knowing that that's going to be a vehicle that you can send your super-signature. Make those offers. Make sure that you know what are the gateways that are going to move people into profit activator #4. What are the things that are going to trigger them taking those next steps? Do that every single week, and you're going to be amazed at what happens.

Now, if you've already got opt-ins, you've already been gathering people's names and emails, you've got a list and you've sent them through your 21-day gauntlet, even just the language. It just kills me, that they send people through the gauntlet, like we're going to scalp them or something. And you don't do anything other than send your JV promotions to them, or whenever you want to sell them something, whenever you communicate with them, you're sitting on a goldmine, and that's your opportunity to reengage with those people by crafting a simple 9-word email.

And that, anybody can do. If you've got more than 50 people on an opt-in list, you can probably do it with 10 people, whatever it is, if you've got anybody, look through your desk drawer. All those scraps of people where you wrote people's name and email down, and all of the people who've emailed you and you haven't done anything with it, or go back in your gmail and look at all the people who inquired 90 days ago, all those kinds of things, gather them all in one place and send them a simple email that says whatever is going to engage people in a dialogue, whatever's going to get them going your way.

So, all you want to do is just send a simple email that's going to get them engaged in dialogue with you, and know where you're going. Know where you're heading. It's really about just skillfully creating that pathway, making it seamless to go from profit activator 2, where you compel them to raise their hand, profit activator 3, where you engage them with a dialogue, educate and motivate them to want to meet with you, so you can make an offer.

Joe: Good stuff. Very good stuff. You did all the talking. That's good. Hope everyone likes it. Hope they go out and make themselves a lot of money.

Dean: Money, money, money.

Joe: And then, send us some. You know, we don't even have a store on I Love Marketing.

Dean: Not yet.

Joe: I think we should, though. I think there should be a store.

Dean: I was just sharing something with Gina. It's all top-secret. It's just hush-hush, for right now.

Joe: Okay, cool.

Dean: But you'll be very pleased.

Joe: Alright, everyone. I hope you enjoyed this. I hope you are a sophisticated, brilliant, stealth, ninja-like email marketer, at this point. If you are not, go back and listen to all of these episodes again, because your future depends on it.

Dean: Yes.

Joe: Seriously. Actually, the future of mankind, I think, depends on the advice being dispensed here.

Dean: It could. It's for the children.

Joe: Yeah. And the children's children. And the children's children.

Dean: Generations.

Joe: Alright, Dean, that's a wrap. Everyone, have a great week, until next week. We'll talk to you then. Please go to ILoveMarketing. Please, go if you want. It's only for your benefit. If you're freaking lazy and you've got different shit to do, then don't.

But if you really want to be on top of things, go there, check out the videos, look at the samples, listen to other episodes, and share this with all your friends. Tweet about this episode. Go to Facebook. Create a whole new social network yourself, and tell people whatever. I don't care.

So, that's it. Have a good day.

Dean: See ya!

# Episode 108
# The one where we share some email marketing results

Dean: Hey, everybody. It's Dean Jackson.

Joe: And Joseph John Polish III.

Dean: Wow.

Joe: That isn't my real name, by the way. There's no third.

Dean: I thought you changed your name to Joe, Joe, Joe, Joe, Joe, Joe Polish.

Joe: Yeah, that's my rapper name.

Dean: There you go.

Joe: We've done a lot of episodes on email and email marketing.

Dean: You could call it a series, really.

Joe: Yeah. It's been good, and people have been happy. We broke it up with a really great episode with Amy Porterfield, who is a Facebook marketing expert.

So, if you've not listened to the episode before this one, then we recommend you go listen to it, because it was really good. Lots of incredible feedback from people I've talked to that have used it. I let a few people that are part of my team and my colleagues listen to it, and now they're using these techniques that we discussed on the last episode, and they're completely changing the way that they...

Dean: We're getting some really great comments and feedback and stuff. Read that one you were telling me from your fan page.

Joe: A guy posted on my fan page. I won't mention his name, but if anyone wants to look up my fan page they can probably find it. It's on Facebook.

It says, "Hey Joe, I didn't want to post this publicly, because I don't want my whole marketing community to see what I just did with your last 3 I Love Marketing podcasts. I've got a list of about 10,000 direct response Internet marketers that, for all intents and purposes, was dead. Using your dialogue technique, I not only doubled my open rates within a week, but I also sent an email that said, "Do you still need marketing help" to everyone who hasn't opened anything in the past 3 months, and I woke that segment up too."

"I'm blown away. Definitely, the most valuable 3 hours I've spent doing anything business-related this week. Just wanted to say thanks."

So, what he's referring to is the most valuable 3 hours that he spent doing anything business-related this week was listening to those 3 episodes.

So, "Cheers, Adam." And he's like, "PS: I found a marketing hack a little while ago, that gave me a massive 250% profit increase and resulted in an opt-in control of 80%. It's the first part of a sales letter, but it's really cool. I think you'll like it." And then, he puts the post for the letter, and then, "PPS: the whole site is being revamped, right now. I've been testing the model for the past 6 months, and it's definitely an ELF business, which stands for Easy, Lucrative and Fun."

That is fantastic. This is a person who is implementing what we are talking about on the podcasts. Of course, I've got to give you credit, because you've been doing most of the talking on those episodes, and I just kind of sit back and drink tea and listen to you pontificate, and throw in a sarcastic comment here and there.

What ends up at the end is a very good instruction on how people can make money using email, how to better communicate, how to create more response.

So, what we'll do, since there's been such a good response to this and the people who have been listening have gotten so much value out of it, we'll use this episode to sort of wrap it up and add any more insights, perspectives, and comments.

Dean: What's great is that we've got Mary Ellen, this week, Mary Ellen Tribby.

Joe: Yeah. She'll be the next episode.

Dean: Absolutely. What a great thing, because who better than Mary Ellen Tribby, somebody who's built an empire using email? This is a great finale to the series, really.

Joe: Yep. So, good stuff happening at I Love Marketing. And people are thinking, "Oh, you would just run out of content." Well, I don't think so.

Dean: That's so funny. I love it. There's another comment on the web page, on the comments on episode 106. This is pretty cool. Jeff Johnson said, "Hey guys, after the I Love Marketing event, Robin and I sent out one of your 9-word emails, like this, for our producer's club coaching program, and it generated more than 20 warm leads, 15 new members at $14,000+ per year, and generated 120 responses to the email out of 700 emailed out. Wow! That was the Friday of I Love Marketing 2, and now I need to send one again."

Interesting, huh?

Joe: Totally.

Dean: I just love these kinds of things. When I really look at things, if you've got anybody who has opted-in or responded to anything, at any time, and haven't yet bought, you have a goldmine. You really do. It's absolutely crazy.

Just reactivating those people, using those short emails, there's a goldmine in your profit activator #3. Once they've crossed that line, they've identified themselves, they cool up in profit activator #3, waiting for you to make a killer offer that's going to move them into your during unit.

Joe: Right. Let's take this message that's on my fan page, where he sent out an email that says, "Do you still need marketing help?" If you are in the marketing business, "Do you need marketing help?" If you are a massage therapist, "Do you still need a massage? Do you still have tension in your neck?" whatever it is. It doesn't much matter. It's just a real simple sort of communication.

I think everyone, myself included, probably violates this to a certain degree. When I mean violates, this whole principle of knowing that it's whatever the number is. For different studies and things that I've read over the years from the Direct Marketing Association – and this goes back to when I first started learning marketing, about how it's 5 or 6 times more expensive to get a new customer than it is to resell to an existing one. There are different studies.

Who the hell even really knows what the exact number is? And I'm sure it's different per industry, and all that. But the bottom line is anyone that understands lifetime value of a client knows that one of the most expensive costs in business is client acquisition, getting them the first time, and then getting them to buy over and over again is better.

A lot of companies – and, again, I say myself in this – will become very good at the before unit and getting customers, and it's more exciting to chase after new customers. You can have really happy clients that buy from you over and over again, and both me and you certainly have that. And at this point in our careers, even if we don't do much of anything, other than continuing to provide value, we're going to have people that have done so well with what we sell them that they will continue to give us money and do business with us.

That being said, you can get into this mode where your new customers, new acquisition, and you have people that are being neglected or people that you could communicate with more frequently, or you could send them a 9-word email, and you don't because you get caught up chasing new customers.

Sometimes, you could turn off – not that I would ever recommend it, I'm just saying – all of these other activities that you're trying to do, these new products, these new whatever, and just simply look at who's given us money in the past that we have not really communicated with as effectively as we could.

A lot of times, you will make more profits by quit trying to chase after new people and just do a damned good job with the ones you've already got.

That also applies not just to repeat business; it also applies to referrals, because you can use this methodology just to get existing people to refer you more.

Dean: I'm glad you said that. That's something that that is a big focus that most people overlook. They don't think about that, at the very beginning.

Just about a month ago now, in February, we have an event here in Orlando for our Moneymaking Websites clients. We do an Internet Academy weekend. So, I recorded an audio program that was like my top 10 breakthrough ideas, because this year marks 25 years that I've been in real estate. I got my real estate license in 1988, and now we're 25 years later. I can't believe that!

I thought about it, and I started outlining my ideas in the order that I would start applying them. The first idea was know your numbers. Most of the time, people don't have a sense of even the basic metrics about where their business is coming from, what's working, how much they're spending, how much they're making, just even basic metrics for their before unit, their during unit and their after unit.

So, the awareness that we had, after talking about that and going around the room, kind of having people share, the main awareness that we had about it was that they don't have an awareness of it. And that's okay. That's an awareness in itself. Just to know that start measurement stuff, it's just such a well-known thing that whatever you measure improves, and whatever you measure and record improves exponentially.

So, it's about measuring the right things. One of the things that we measure is the ROI in your after unit, and there's really no equivalent.

I was just talking to the fitness twins in London today, and they've really embraced this after unit. They do personal training facilities, 2 of them, in the UK. They've started sending the equivalent of the world's most interesting postcard to their clients, to their existing clients.

Their ROI on sending things to their clients is over 2,000%, 2,200% - 22 times what they spend is how much revenue they've brought in on doing those things.

So, we talk about doing these short, personal, expecting-a-reply emails, if you're sending them to people who actually already know you, and you're sending a personal email to them, and you're doing it in a way that's going to be right in their wheelhouse for orchestrating referrals. It's such an incredible opportunity. Most people don't ever focus on that first. Everybody focuses on the before unit and getting those things in place. That's all the fun and the newness and the excitement of testing and spending money on ads, and all that kind of stuff.

But, the real value, the highest ROI, the no-brainer money is in your after unit, orchestrating referrals, and in moving people from profit activator #3, making offers, engaging with them, and getting them into your during unit. Those are the 2 hidden goldmines that you have right there, in your business. Everybody's got them.

It's almost like magic tricks. It's almost like when I start with somebody, those are the first 2 things I look at. What can we do to create a magic trick for them? And, if they have prospects they haven't communicated with or haven't communicated with in a real intelligent way, there's the big opportunity. Just react to those people.

Joe: The thing is most people do not send out monthly client newsletters. I even recently found – this is what happens when you grow a big organization and, like a dumbass, don't have systems in place to make sure that proven things that work continue to stay doing them – kind of like a system, once you set up a system properly, it doesn't need constant monitoring. Maybe a little bit of maintenance but, for the most part, a complete system, once you set it up, it just works. You don't have to keep going and fixing it, and that sort of thing.

There are things that I've set up pretty well in my company, and a lot of things that I have not set up well or not set up a mechanism for me to be reminded of.

I have found, recently, that there are people that have given me money in the past, that have not done business in a while and, for whatever reason, were taken off of certain mailing lists.

I ultimately have to be responsible for this, because it's my company, my organization. So, even if one of my employees made a dumbass mistake – which, in some cases I've had that happen a lot – the real dumbass responsibility lies on my shoulders, because it happened while I was obviously owning the company.

There are people that have not been communicated with that, if they would have been, frequently, they would continue to get back onboard and continue to do business with, and things like that. And I've just made this recent discovery of quite a bit of communication that has not happened, and it's one of those things to where there are a lot of activities going on in my company, where we're getting prospects, we're getting new customers, we're getting new clients, and all that sort of thing.

At the same time, we're having to spend money to do that, that is much higher than the money spent to send a newsletter to a past client, send an email to a past client, make a phone call to past clients.

So, this applies to everybody. I don't care how great someone is, there are places in their business that – hopefully – listening to this episode will just make them stop and think, "Okay, where could I apply this method?" Instead of saying, "Oh, I don't know if this will work for me," of "I'm just going to listen to this episode while I'm working out, for entertainment purposes," if you're really listening to this, where could you apply it? Where are areas in your business where there is some neglect, some lack of communication, some place where you have really even sent out a long-form compelling sales letter that's direct response? Well, you think it is, but maybe you can try this 9-word email or 5-word email, or whatever it is, on a particular area, and put some attention on it?

If you just think about that for a couple of minutes, most people, if they were to write it down, could come up with 5 or 10 areas immediately. Anyway, that's what I'm saying.

Dean: It's really interesting, because I get a lot of feedback from people. They send out emails, and they don't know where it's headed. They just get a 9-word email, they throw out 9 words, and get somebody to respond, and they're saying, "Oh, I got all these responses," but then they don't know where they're headed with it.

So, you've got to know what the end result is, I always say, how to think like a chess master. In order to think like a chess master, you've got to kind of know where you're steering it. If your goal is to get to the end in 3 moves, you've got to know where the end is, so you can reverse-engineer back.

So, everything kind of leads to a logical next step. And that's why, sometimes, when we start with a sorting question, like asking somebody, "Are you whatever?" or something that's going to get them to respond kind of yes or no, or make a choice of this or that, you've got to know that if they respond this, that you now take the next step that's going to kind of deepen that conversation and then offer and steer towards your solution, so that they can get this.

And if they answer that, then you deepen that and point to the solution that's going to help them get that.

And just knowing those things really are about just setting the stage to offer your cookies, offer the next step, the things that are the result of thinking through what your prospect's conversations are. What are the conversations that are going on in their head? What are they going to need next? What's going to trigger them to take that action? And how can I present it in a way that just seems so natural that it doesn't feel like I'm even making this big commitment or decision, that it just seems like, "Of course, I want that." That's the natural next step.

Joe: Right. Here's the thing. Like when you're saying, "The natural next step," it's kind of like the way of the slippery slide conversation, about the greased shoot. You've heard all of these analogies from copywriters. How do you keep people moving through the process, because everything is the natural next step? Not the forced next step, not the manipulated them into a sales pitch next step, but what do people want and how do you provide it to them and get them to continue to go? How do you talk to them? What do you say? How do you say it?

Have you ever read *Obvious Adams* or whatever that book is?

Dean: Yeah, right.

Joe: It's kind of like that. We should just read that book out loud one day. It's really short. It would take up a whole

|       |                                                                                                                                                                                                                                                                                                                                                                                                                                                                                                                                                                                                                                                                          |
|-------|----------------------------------------------------------------------------------------------------------------------------------------------------------------------------------------------------------------------------------------------------------------------------------------------------------------------------------------------------------------------------------------------------------------------------------------------------------------------------------------------------------------------------------------------------------------------------------------------------------------------------------------------------------------------------|
|       | episode. If we run out of shit to talk about, we can just get really short books.                                                                                                                                                                                                                                                                                                                                                                                                                                                                                                                                                                                          |
| Dean: | That could probably happen. Let's schedule it in for episode 700.                                                                                                                                                                                                                                                                                                                                                                                                                                                                                                                                                                                                          |
| Joe:  | We'll do like bedtime reading, and we'll just read marketing books to people. We'll say, "Play these to your children early on, so that when they…"                                                                                                                                                                                                                                                                                                                                                                                                                                                                                                                        |
| Dean: | How great would that be?                                                                                                                                                                                                                                                                                                                                                                                                                                                                                                                                                                                                                                                   |
| Joe:  | You never know.                                                                                                                                                                                                                                                                                                                                                                                                                                                                                                                                                                                                                                                            |
| Dean: | I know.                                                                                                                                                                                                                                                                                                                                                                                                                                                                                                                                                                                                                                                                    |
| Joe:  | There's going to be some technology, 50 years ago, and someone's going to be listening to I Love Marketing, and they're going to be like, "Remember when there was direct mail? Remember those days when there was that thing called the 'Internet'? Now, you just think and messages pop up into your head. Computers are pretty much tied into your brain and everything. They'll probably have 3D imagery that just makes your… Now I'm going to sound totally insane here. But where they're going to be thinking, and then I'll be talking, and it will be through like Batman, and then you'll be talking, and there will be like a Robin figure sort of thing. That's just how it's going to be delivered. |
| Dean: | Uh-huh.                                                                                                                                                                                                                                                                                                                                                                                                                                                                                                                                                                                                                                                                    |
| Joe:  | Are you following where I'm going with this?                                                                                                                                                                                                                                                                                                                                                                                                                                                                                                                                                                                                                               |
| Dean: | I am. Absolutely.                                                                                                                                                                                                                                                                                                                                                                                                                                                                                                                                                                                                                                                          |
| Joe:  | Now, you're not. I'm just babbling.                                                                                                                                                                                                                                                                                                                                                                                                                                                                                                                                                                                                                                        |
| Dean: | It's constant evolution. I was going to read another comment.                                                                                                                                                                                                                                                                                                                                                                                                                                                                                                                                                                                                              |
| Joe:  | Alright, go ahead.                                                                                                                                                                                                                                                                                                                                                                                                                                                                                                                                                                                                                                                         |

Dean: This is interesting, because this will have a little discussion we can have.

So, "Dean and Joe, last 3 episodes about email were classic. I love how you appeal to the reader's self-interest. Enclosed are 3 emails I'm considering sending to my list. I also enclosed my best cold email template. These are the emails I'm considering sending."

"Oh, a little background on my list. My company helps you connect with hard-to-reach people through a cold email. We focus on entrepreneurs who are looking for joint ventures in businesses whose customers spend $50,000 or more. So, these are the emails I'm considering sending. Email one, 'Are you still looking for customers using email?' What do you think about that one – 8 words? If you add your name, there are 9."

I think there's something very valuable about the word still. If you're saying, "Are you still looking for customers using email?" especially if you can put that message on top of your reply to their inquiry months ago.

A lot of times, they might forget something or you just want to kind of anchor back that they asked for something, that's one of the cool things that I've often used as a strategy for these short emails. Rather than just sending them alone, I'll send them in reply to an email that I may have sent them months ago. So, if they inquire about something, that adds an anchor back to "Are you still looking for customers using email, like you were when you inquired 8 months ago or 90 days ago?" or whatever.

This is pretty interesting, because I've used a lot of these emails, the short, engaging emails, as a follow-up right after they've opted-in. So, I think like a 1-2 combination. We talked, last week, about this idea of the matrix of when people actually convert. If we're saying that 50% of them who inquire are actually going to buy something in the next 18 months, but only 15% of them are going to do it in the first 90 days, and 85% after 90 days.

So, our main focus, initially, is on identifying who are the people who are going to do something now. Who are those 15% that we can approach right now? So, when they opt-in, I like to send something immediately, as an autoresponse that looks like it is an autoresponse. I'm not trying to fool somebody into thinking that I sent them a personal email at 2:30 in the morning, 10 seconds after they opted-in for something.

When it clearly is an autoresponder message, I don't ever try to put that off as a personal message. When you send that, it can be a welcome. It's like, "Here's the link to what you've downloaded or where to download what you just opted-in for, and here are some ways I can help you," and you're kind of setting the stage.

It's like the welcome email. Kind of get them everything that they need to know. In case they want to do something now, here's what you do.

And then the next day, on top of that message, so I'm sending that message again, with a subject line of "re," whatever that is, and then using that short, sorting message.

I shared, a few episodes ago, that combination with Vince Del Monte, using an opt-in on his website and sending out a message that asks people, "Are you looking to gain muscle or lose fat?"

When people reply, now you're engaged in that dialogue with them.

But then, it hit me that people could reply, and you could get into a dialogue with them. And if you're skillful and you know where you're headed, if somebody says, "I'm interested in fat loss," then you've got the next dialogue that you're leading them towards a completely risk-free offer, all cheese/no whiskers, to try your product that's going to get them the goal of losing fat.

Now, not everybody who you present that to, if you present it to them skillfully, you'll get as many as you can, but not everybody will. And at 90 days, it's probably a good idea to send a message that follows back up with them if they didn't buy.

So, if somebody says, "I'm looking to lose fat," or "I'm looking to gain muscle," and your next reply to them is, "That's great! How many pounds are you looking to gain?" and now you're engaged in this dialogue with them and they say, "Well, I'd like to gain 20 pounds of muscle," and you're steering them towards the program that you have. "You know what would be great for you? It's my no-nonsense muscle-building program, and here's the thing all about it." You're steering them towards exactly what they need and making it easy for them to take you up on that.

But if you get that far and they don't buy, and they told you that they wanted to gain 20 pounds of muscle, sometimes they don't buy because they're maybe going to try something else, and maybe yours didn't win that time. They're hot to gain muscle. They told you that they were. And they didn't buy your product, so there must be something that they've done, or they've done nothing, and 90 days later, or 60 days later, if you send a reply to that same message that they responded back, and you say, "Hey, Joe, just checking in. How many pounds of muscle have you gained so far?" and they haven't gained any, now you're re-engaged in that dialogue at the 90-day mark, and you can start that whole process again.

But you've got to know where it's headed.

I use that as an example, but it's the same. You talk about the glop. Gaining muscle is the glop. Whatever their glop is, whatever it is that they want to do, you want to determine, "Do you want this or do you want that?"

So, when we ask the people who inquire on the real estate websites, "Are you an investor or are you looking for a house to live in?" that's an and/or question.

Joe: Based on the little bit of dialogue that's been going on here that you've been saying, I wrote down some words as I've been sitting here, that you have said.

A lot of times, in conversations, I think a lot of people miss how much is being discussed on this particular topic. I'm just going to read some of the words that you said. Okay?

Dean: Okay.

Joe: As it relates to using email and communicating, and doing it in a very simple way.

Anchor back. So, anchoring people back to a previous communication.

Sent in reply to a past email.

Inquire about.

These are all of the activities that are happening when people are communicating and engaging with you. Some of these will just be one word that could be in the context of the email or could be just describing what your suggesting/recommending/persuading/advising/offering people to do.

One is try. Identify their goal. Present to them skillfully. Timing. Follow-up (if they don't buy). Next reply. Engaged in a dialogue. Steer them towards exactly what they need, and make it easy for them. Checking in. Re-engage. Process, and determine do you want this or that?

Those are some of the words that you said. But I think if anyone was just to break down those words, like, "Okay, you have a bunch of people, or maybe a handful, that have inquired. They have inquired. There's interest on some level.

Now, have you made it easy for them to try what it is you're doing? Have you identified their goal? Have you presented it to them skillfully? Have you done it in the right timing? Are you following-up with them if they don't buy? Are you making a note to yourself to follow-up? Are you building it into your autoresponder, into your database? And if you don't have a complicated database and you're doing everything out of gmail or Outlook, are you putting a reminder on your calendar to do that, if you don't have software like Infusionsoft, as an example? Are you engaging in a dialogue with them? Are you steering them towards exactly what they want, not what you think they want or need, but what they actually think they want and need? And are you making it easy for them?

Are you checking in with them? Instead of treating people like they're just these people you never meet in person, if you care about them, are you checking in with them? And if they dropped off because, like you were saying, it wasn't a right fit, are you reengaging them? And are you building this into just a process of how you do business? Are you determining "Do you want this or that? Do you not want this or that?"

All of these things can be figured out. There are a million other things I could have written here, but I just wanted to do this for a few minutes, just to bring it back to how much is here that people may overlook. They may hear you saying these things, but I want them to really think about the psychology of what is being discussed here. This is really powerful, important, useful stuff. And stuff is a technical term.

Dean: It really is. Yeah. What's the unit of measurement of stuff?

Joe: It's a lot.

Dean: It's a ton of stuff. Yeah.

Joe: So, this episode is not just about something you should do this week or next week, or this month, this is something that you want to be doing all the time, for the rest of your business career.

The business owners that are listening to these email episodes, this also could be done not just email. I've talked about this before, in the past, but I have a friend named Jim. Not high school, but right out of high school, he was friends with a lot of people I went to high school with, which I hang out with none of those people anymore, but me and Jim are friends.

There had been a period of time where we had talked on the phone a couple times, but had not seen each other, literally not seen each other in person in over a decade. And when I was doing my first annual 25K meeting in LA was the first time that I did an annual 25K meeting. I think you were there. I had Dean Graziosi, Bill Phillips, Richard Branson, Dan Sullivan come and talk at it. Tim Ferriss was there. Actually, Tim's been at every one of my annual 25K meetings, except one.

I'd sent a text message to this guy saying, "Hey, check out this website. I've got some pretty awesome speakers. Let me know if you want to go." It was a text message. And he sends me back another text, "Yes, I'd like to go and take one of my friends." It was $10,000 a person. We did an episode on it, I think. Maybe I'm delusional. But if you remember this, when I was talking about how I made $20,000 sale from a text message from a friend, simply by making an offer, and then it dawned on me that, "Wow, you could actually run an entire business off an iPhone, if you have the right words.

Dean: That's absolutely true, because the short messages are the ones that seem like they're the real deal.

Joe: Right. Now, I do audio messages, I do video, but I do it to the right people, at the right time, with the right offer, in the right way.

But, you know what? Who cares what I do? That's what anyone listening to us is going to do if they're going to have results. And if they don't do those things, they're not going to get results.

This isn't overly complicated. I think it's really complicated if someone really doesn't kind of get and understand marketing.

So, I think the more you study the psychology of marketing and the more people read the Claude Hopkins books and the Robert Collier letter books, and all of the old, awesome, principle-based direct response books, I think the more all this stuff that seems to need complications and a lot of setup, it's like, "Look, just treat people the way they want to be treated. Deliver them what it is they want. Think about things from their perspective, and realize it's not just the before unit that you should be spending your attention on. It's the during unit. It's the after unit.

If you have all of these, it's the 3-legged stool. You take any of them away; you're going to have problems.

Dean: Uh-huh.

Joe: Well, you're going to have problems. Fuck it; you're going to have problems. I shouldn't say you won't have problems. You will not realize all of the profits you can and will, and the referrals, and all the other things that go along with it, if you don't get this down.

Dean: Right. I was thinking about, as you were talking, what would be my sequence, what I would have people do. I think if you've been listening to this series, you've invested the time, you've heard tale after tale of strategies and different examples of what people have done using email, I really think it comes down to now just deciding that you're going to take action.

You hear these comments from people who have tried it. It doesn't take very long to actually do it, but they've done it, and it's universally a big hit when you reengage with your prospects.

The 3 basic things that I think everybody can do are: 1) reengage with the people who already in profit activator #3. Everybody who you haven't had any communication with in 90 days, just do that. You never know. You could be sitting on a goldmine. You're certainly sitting on an immediate cash infusion into your business. If you've been generating leads and you've been putting people through your 21-day gauntlet, and then sending them to the archive, where you're not really communicating with them anymore, and you write them off as bad leads, then you've got this opportunity to reengage with all of those people.

It always ranges from thousands, on the low end of dollars that are right there, waiting for you to capture it, all the way up on the high end, with our friend Phillip Bell, the yacht broker, who sent out the 9-word email to yacht inquirers and is under contract on a $120-million custom yacht build, joking that the 9-word email got a 9-figure client.

So, it ranges in there. You heard us just reading the comments of somebody who got – I forget how many they said – 20 $14,000 clients from reengaging with people by sending out that 9-word email.

So, that's just sitting there waiting for you, right now. That would be where I would immediately start.

Joe: I was going to say we also have that one guy who sent out the 9-word email at the 2-day conference we were doing last year, that evening, and came back the next day and he had made $100,000 in sales.

Dean: Right. Exactly.

Joe: Literally, overnight.

Dean: Yeah, exactly. And I've had that at Breakthrough Blueprint events, people sending out an email on day one and then making thousands of dollars just in the time that we're right there at the event.

You're right, it's fast-acting, it's something that is there, and it's something that you can go back and do again and again and again. You can send it every month, to everybody who's been in more than 90 days.

A lot of times, people send something like the gentleman that said that they got the 20 $14,000 clients from it, that was actually at the I Love Marketing event that they did that. And he said, "Yeah, it's probably time that we do it again." And you're right, because that was October. So, we're like, "That's November, December, January, February, March. That's 6 months ago."

Joe: See, what happens is people actually forget just how quickly time passes, and they just don't do it.

You've heard me say this a bunch of times. I think one of the roles that we play in people's lives is we're just a reminder service.

Dean: That's probably true, yeah.

Joe: And I've had people that are brilliant marketers, that listen to all of our I Love Marketing episodes, and I've had a couple of people tell me, "What I like about I Love Marketing is I know most of what you guys talk about, because I teach it, study it too. It just reminds me to do the things that I know to do but I forget to do, or that I used to do that I quit doing. It's reminding people what to do.

Dean: It's pretty funny.

Joe: Yeah.

Dean: I think they just like to listen and hear us bicker.

Joe: Yeah. I sit and try to be so pleasant.

Dean: That's true. I'm the instigator, always.

Joe: Oh, my god. You were talking about let me go through the process, and you started with reengage. Let's use me.

Dean: That's #1. Everybody should do that. I'm guaranteeing that the next 10 minutes of just this episode is going to be worth thousands of dollars to you. I can't imagine anybody that it's not going to be worth thousands of dollars to.

Joe: I can tell you who those people are: people who won't do jack shit. Or, worse, people that aren't hearing this.

Dean: That's true. If a tree falls in the forest... That's right.

Joe: Right. If marketing wisdom is dispensed, but you are not there to hear it, you are destined for bankruptcy.

Dean: Oh, that's so funny.

Joe: Maybe.

Dean: And true.

Joe: Yep.

Dean: The second thing that I would do is immediately start communicating with your after unit, with the people who already know you, like you and trust you. You can do that by email. The #1 thing that you can certainly do is start orchestrating referrals, reengaging with your clients, just paying attention to all the stuff that's going on, and just asking, in a real simple way that makes all the sense in the world. It's clear that you're just sending it to them, because you know them. They're already your clients. They're not surprised to hear from you. It's not coming out of the blue. Hopefully, it's not coming out of the blue. Hopefully, it hasn't been years since you even communicated with them.

If that's the case, then certainly a short, personal, expecting-a-reply email is a great way to reengage with people, if you haven't had any kind of engagement with them.

A lot of times, people are reluctant to start communicating with their after unit because they've been embarrassingly neglecting them. They haven't really had any communication with them. Lost touch with them. It would feel awkward for them to, all of a sudden, start asking for referrals.

So, I agree with that. I think a great way to start is just by reconnecting with them.

I often say, to the realtors, "Just pay attention to where you're driving during the day. And if you drive by, it doesn't even have to be their street or their house, it could be their neighborhood, but if I drove down the street where your little neighborhood is, Joe, and we hadn't spoken in a while, I might just send you a quick email and say, "Hey Joe, I just drove by your place the other day, and it reminded me I haven't talked to you in a while. How are you doing?" That kind of short, reengaging thing. You know?

You'd be surprised how many people would respond to something like that. They got busy, too. They maybe feel bad that they haven't kept in touch with you.

Joe: That's a really good point. A lot of times, people have this perception that, "Oh, I'm bothering."

You know the whole thing, and it was more prevalent, but it still exists today, but it was more prevalent in the beginning, when all of this email marketing was first being done, and I used to hear it all the time with newsletters, "I don't want to mail a newsletter to my carpet cleaning clients every month because they don't get their carpets cleaned except once a year, once every 6 months, or whatever, and I don't want to annoy them." People would be like, "Oh, my god!"

There were actually idiots that would try to knock me off, compete with me, and they'd be like, "Some marketers," and they wouldn't mention my name, of course, because I was the top person in the industry, but they would try to position themselves. They'd be like, "Some marketers will tell you that you should mail a communication to your customer every month, but that's annoying. It really should be every 90 days." And they would try to position themselves, which, of course, is stupid.

Then it becomes email, where you can actually send an email out, and people are like, "Oh, you can't email your clients once a week! That's annoying!"

We have our monthly ezine. I remember when all of this first started. Then, we find people that will email their clients twice a day, and they have a great following and they'll have tons of success with it, while another person is like, "Once a week is way too much," and I always had to ask myself, "Well, yeah, if I didn't like the person and they were smothering me, as a friendship, not like a business – you'd take this in a personal relationship – if you really have a great friend, if you have someone that you really like, when they contact you or call you, if this person really adds value to your life, you actually like hearing from them, especially if they're offering things that you like.

Now, because there's money being transacted, people somehow confuse the fact that if they really like your food and every time they buy it, they consume it and they buy more, they actually probably like hearing from you on a regular basis.

What you think is going on in their world may be completely different than what's going on in their world. And if they're super-busy and they're not responding to your weekly email, and you're thinking, "Oh, they're probably not responding because I'm emailing them too frequently," it might be just because they're busy and they happened to miss that one.

You take Gaping Void, by Hugh McLeod, they mail out a daily email, and I usually read it or look at the artwork. Seth Goden also has a really good daily email.

Dean: Right.

Joe: That sort of stuff. But there are other people that have daily emails that I'll subscribe to but I really don't read, but every once in a while I will.

And then, there are other people that I never hear from at all. And if they do send me something, I feel like, "You probably should have been doing this more frequently, because you kind of forgot I existed."

I have all kinds of clients and people that have opted-in all in between, in terms of the frequency and when and how I communicate, and things like that.

But the point is that if you have great rapport with somebody, then they probably not only appreciate hearing from you, they're probably going to respond favorably. And if they're not, then either there's something wrong with what you're delivering, your glop, to use the glop term, or there's something wrong with the way you're saying it, the way you're communicating, which is why we've been talking about how to actually communicate in the ways that have been proven to be most effective.

This whole 9-word email, you really made the discovery on this sort of stuff, just because of how much of a simplistic breaking down of complexity thinker that you are. None of what's being talked about on these episodes here, these are not like opinions. All of this stuff has been tested over and over and over again, before we decided to do an episode and talk about email marketing.

Dean: Right.

Joe: None of this is opinion. This is proven to work. This is the most effective ways to reengage and communicate with your clients, if your intended purpose is to get a result and to get a response, and to get people to reengage.

Dean: Yeah.

Joe: I was talking to this website company, Yazamo, who actually is here in my building. They're really great guys that build websites. Yazamo.com. They give portions of their money to Kiva, and all kinds of cool stuff. They just quoted a guy, who has a pretty successful business, on building a direct response website, and they were telling me that they had just paid a company $100,000 to build a website for them that has produced like nothing.

The funny thing is the amount of advice we have given on the last – this being the fourth in this particular series – on email marketing is worth 1,000 times more than this website that this company just paid $100,000 to have developed in the hopes that it would position and sell what it is they're selling.

But I'll tell you, it would be easier for the company's owner to get a really fancy proposal from a company that dresses it up and makes it sound good and proposes to spend $100,000, and make that investment, than it would be to sit down for 4 hours and actually think through the psychology of how you're communicating to current, past clients and customers and prospects through simple emails.

Dean: Right. And that's the thing. What's almost ridiculous is how ridiculous these seem. Like the last episode in the series was ridiculously easy strategies. They seem ridiculously easy, but they're so thought-out, they're definitely beginning with the end in mind. You're heading towards something.

So, they're saying just the right words to get just the right action, one action at a time. We don't have to get them to take 3 steps at once. You only have to get them to take one step, the next step. That's the only thing that you want to focus on. You want to always lead to the next step.

So, I was talking about the after unit of just reconnecting with people, but that, with the end being that you're communicating regularly with them and adding value to their lives, not that you're just coming out of left field all of a sudden to start asking for referrals or to start asking for help, or seeing if they know somebody.

Those kinds of things, what really makes those effective is when you have a close relationship with people – when they're current; when you're on their mind.

So, that's like you've got to have kind of the barrier to entry, to doing that, that you've got some level of current relationship with them.

So, the best way to get back into a current relationship with someone is to just send them a short email that you were thinking about them or saying hi, or connecting somehow.

Joe: Yep. In the time we have left, I would, for my own selfish purposes, because I think it would be instructive, plus I think it's a good way to break it down, and I want people to see just how – I kind of know the answers to this, and I already know some of the things I'm going to send – what would you do if you were me?

Here I'm a guy that knows a boatload about marketing. I've sold a lot of products to people in the past, that are knowledge products, they're sales letters and templates and tools on how to do marketing, I've run coaching programs, I have things like Nightingale-Conant programs, you know all the different stuff that I sell, and I have people on my list that have given me money and a lot of people that have made a boatload of money, but one year they're not able to make an event or do coaching, or whatever, and they just drop out.

What would I send to them? What would be an example, if you were me, and you found, in your database, that there are people that I'm communicating with, what would be an example of what you would say to them? What would the subject line be? We've already talked about this already.

Dean: So, we're talking about carpet cleaners?

Joe: Yep. Let's say carpet cleaners. It could be anyone on my list, which you know. But let's, for the sake of the conversation and keeping it simple for people listening, I'm going to send something to carpet cleaning clients to reengage them, because I have not communicated with them in a while. What would I say?

Dean: What do you want them to do? That would be the first question. So, you start thinking about you've got all these people. First of all, you need to be able to separate them out from the herd. You've got this list of let's say it's 1,000 people. Maybe it's more. Probably more. But let's say there are 1,000.

Joe: Let me play this, then. I don't know what I want them to do, Dean.

Dean: That's what you've got to know. It's almost like the Cheshire Cat. If you don't know where you're headed, then any road will get you there. Right?

Joe: Right. Exactly. So, I don't know what to do. Should I put them on a teleseminar? I have this new upgrade kit, which is my carpet cleaner's course that's updated for this year, which is true, by the way. And it's got the latest updated marketing strategies for carpet cleaners.

Dean: So, what's one of the strategies that you've got that's new, that would be a magic trick for me?

Joe: How to make money with Google AdWords.

Dean: So, do a lot of carpet cleaners have a website?

Joe: Yes, some do. Some do not. And most of them have lousy websites.

Dean: They do?

Joe: And we do have websites for cleaners that actually work.

Dean: So, if some of them don't, or they don't even have that yet, it could be as simple as asking a simple question, just saying, "Hey Joe, what's your website?" or "Do you have a website?" Do you have a website? All we're doing is we're kind of engaging, because it's about the Web and about the thing.

This is a dialogue method. So, what you have the opportunity to do is take the information that you get in response to your reaching out, and you can build on that information and steering it into a direction.

So, if you don't have something that's going to show them, and if you've got a model that works, that's something new that you've been doing, you've been working on a great lead generating website for carpet cleaners, you've got a model that you've recently set up.

One of the things that you might do, when somebody replies with their website, is you might say something like, "That's perfect! Can I use your website in a Web clinic? I'm going to put together a Web clinic video," or something like that, where now you're engaging there and you're also doing something that is going to create curiosity about what's coming next. You're building anticipation. You're going to use their website in this web clinic type of thing.

This is a strategy that I've actually used, instead of for carpet cleaners, for real estate agents. So, you go through and you've got all of these principles that are what your website is based on – same principles as mine. So, I've got the formula for Internet marketing, which is eyeballs + emails + hearts = faces.

So, you get to meet people. You've got to get their eyeballs; you've got to get their email address. You've got to bond with them. And then the equal sign represents that transition out of the cyber world and into the real world, where you get to meet with them and you're in their living room, cleaning their carpet, or they're in your car, looking for a house.

So, you now have an opportunity to do a Web clinic that shows and illustrates all of those principles in action.

So, you're saying we're going to talk about the formula for Internet marketing for carpet cleaners, and you're going to illustrate the big mistakes that people are making by showing the sites that people have submitted sort of thing for this. So, you're using their websites as examples that most people make the website about themselves. And you start with the domain name, and you show that it's whatever the name, Joe's Carpet Cleaning. For the realtors, it's JoePolish.com or JoeSellsHouses.com, or CallJoeAndStartPacking.com, all of those things that are showing and demonstrating that you are the center and the star of the website.

And then, you contrast that by showing your best idea around that. You're showing how being outwardly focused is actually a bigger win, because that's when you get people to your website.

And then you're going to show another mistake people make is that they're not getting email addresses. They've just got all the information about their site, and then you can show how your website, its soul purpose is to get somebody to raise their hand, to leave their name and their email address.

If you skillfully did that over a period of time, you can go through and show a lot of different websites. And then when somebody replies to that, you're now inviting them to watch the video or come to the webinar, if you're going to do it live, where you stream those things. And they're going to be very interested in it, because you're going to send them an email that says, "Hey, thanks for letting me use your website. Here's the video that I put together using it." And now, they're going to watch that.

Joe: Okay, so we have covered some really awesome stuff here. We are at the time, and we need to wrap up the wrap-up episode.

So, now that we've discussed all of this stuff, what should everyone do, other than go back and listen to the last previous episodes another time, and really internalize this?

Dean: There are going to be people who are listening to this, right now, who won't forgive me unless I tell them what the third thing is, and it's a short one. So, it's easy. But I did say there was going to be 3 things.

Number one was sorting and engaging with your prospects, the ones you haven't communicated with. Number 2 was reconnecting with the people in your after unit, if you haven't already done that. And then the third thing that everybody should be doing is a weekly flagship communication, some reason to be in touch with and add value to your prospects, to educate them about the process of doing business with you, and use that education as a carrier for your offers that motivate them to take the next step. It's about not just education; it's about educate and motivate your prospects to take action.

That's the third thing that I would do.

So, just to wrap this up, they should listen to these episodes. Listen with the intent of applying. Like you were sitting there with your pen, writing down the words. But listen to these and take notes, and stop and think, "How does this apply to me? What could I say? How could I communicate with people in a way that's going to get them to engage?"

Joe: Yep. We have this fancy iPad magazine. Why don't you mention that, real quick?

Dean: How fantastic is that? We've got, now, on the iPad newsstand, the ILoveMarketing madcast. It's using the platform that Ed Dale talked about at the I Love Marketing conference, and we've posted up that episode. There's a whole video of Ed's talk that he gave. But that's the platform we're using, where you're doing exactly what Ed talks about. I'm so happy with it. It's got kind of a great overview of everything, all the concepts that we talk about.

This is a perfect launch to get people introduced to the I Love Marketing ways and everything that we talk about.

When you look at the content that we've put out, when I started looking at it all in one place, kind of the greatest hits type of thing, and you look at the interviews with Richard Branson, Tony Robbins, with Tim Ferriss and Gary Vaynerchuk, and all of the best marketing minds, with Dan Kennedy, Frank Kern, Eben Pagan and Jeff Walker, everybody, it's crazy how much stuff is there. It's amazing to me what you can do with these iPad magazines. Every one of those episodes is in there. You can listen to the audio right there. You can click, you can read the transcript right there. It's awesome.

That would be the perfect thing, if you've got friends that you want to introduce to the I Love Marketing kind of philosophies and the I Love Marketing community. That is a fantastic way to do that. Just send them an email. Tell them to check it out on the iPad, and they'll thank you for it. I can't imagine, per pixel, the value of what that information is in that one publication. It's crazy.

Joe: I also want to put a shout-out to all of the people that are running I Love Marketing Meetup groups all over the world. We really appreciate you sharing all of our philosophies and stuff. I know a lot of people have utilized it to create a Genius Network for themselves and to create joint ventures, create a community where people can go and share.

I do know that we need to update the I Love Marketing episodes on the downloadable "How To Run An I Love Marketing Meetup Group," which is free and available online, at ILoveMarketing.com. So, if you want to attend an I Love Marketing Meetup group or you want to start one, you can go to ILoveMarketing.com and see where they're at – a really good thing if there's not one in your community but you want to put together like-minded people. There are tens of thousands of people, hundreds of thousands that listen to I Love Marketing, so there's certainly, mostly likely, unless you're isolated in some weird part of the world where you may not have anyone in your community that listens to I Love Marketing, but there are many cities where there are hundreds of people who listen to I Love Marketing and are part of I Love Marketing Meetup groups.

So, go out there and meet some of these people, because it'll probably be really helpful to you. And start one. We have a whole guideline online that shows you how to set it up, topics to talk about, how to run a meeting, that sort of stuff. That's available for anyone who wants to do it. As of right now, we don't charge anything for that. We just have people do it. Just do it with integrity and don't use it as a disguised pitch to try to recruit people into a multilevel meeting or something. Use it to discuss marketing.

And even if you're multilevel, that doesn't mean you shouldn't be part of the Meetup group. It just means don't use the I Love Marketing Meetup group thing as a way to try to push people into business opportunities. Do it if you're genuinely interested in having great discussions with people wanting to build and grow their companies using the 8 profit activators, and you want to do it to make yourself better.

It's kind of like the best way to remember jokes is as soon as you hear one, go out and tell it to other people. I have people like, "I can't remember jokes." Yeah, because once you hear one, you don't go out and tell it to anyone. And then, you'll forget it, of course.

So, if you can't remember what to do marketing-wise, as soon as you've heard an episode, go out and tell somebody else about it, have a conversation about it, and use it in your own business. Then, you will not forget it. That's how you make all this stuff stick.

That's it, Dean. We'll see everyone next episode, for an awesome episode. You'll be hearing Mary Ellen Tribby, most likely, unless when we record it in a few days, we just don't like it. Then it will just be back to me and Dean.

Dean: We'll edit out her. No, she's going to be awesome. How could it be better?

Joe: Yep. Exactly. Alright, have a good night, good day, wherever you're at. Get busy sending out some emails.

Dean: Bye.

Made in the USA
Middletown, DE
12 January 2018